WONDERFUL

WILD

WYOMING'S

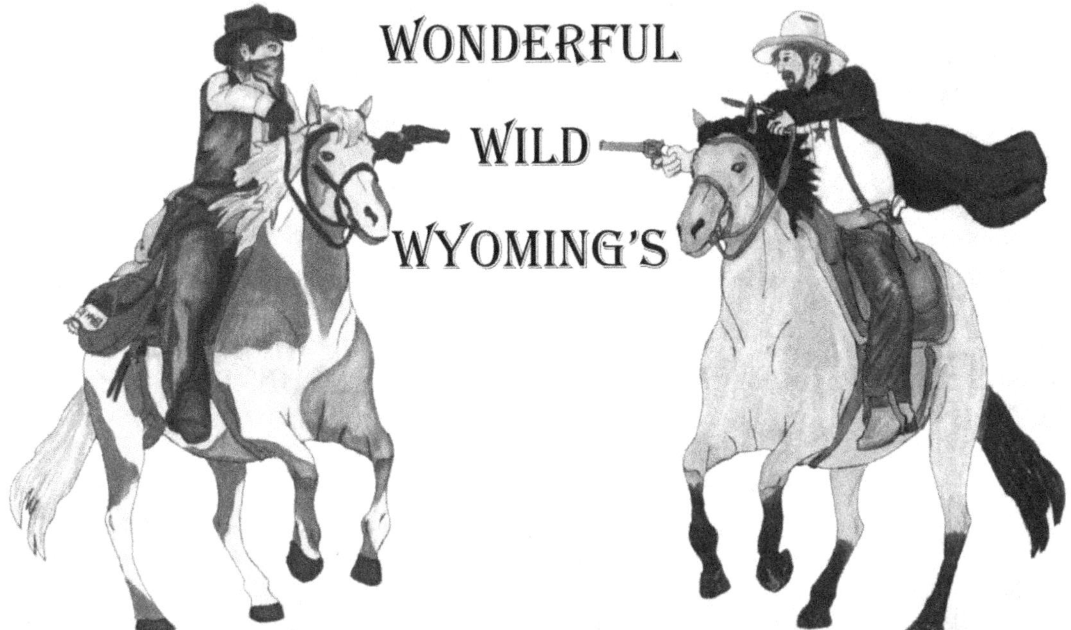

WILD WEST

CLASSIC COLORING BOOK

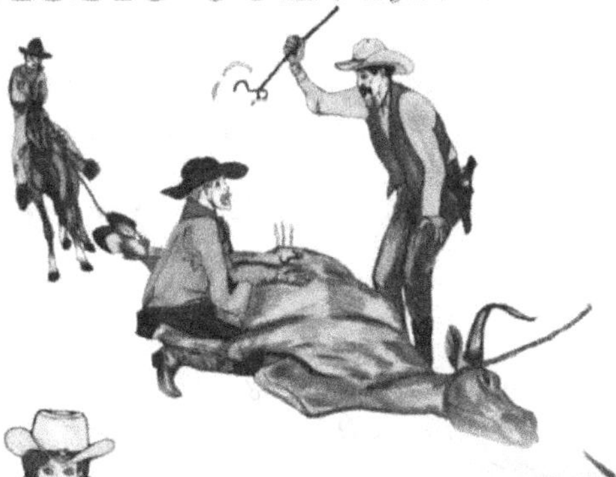

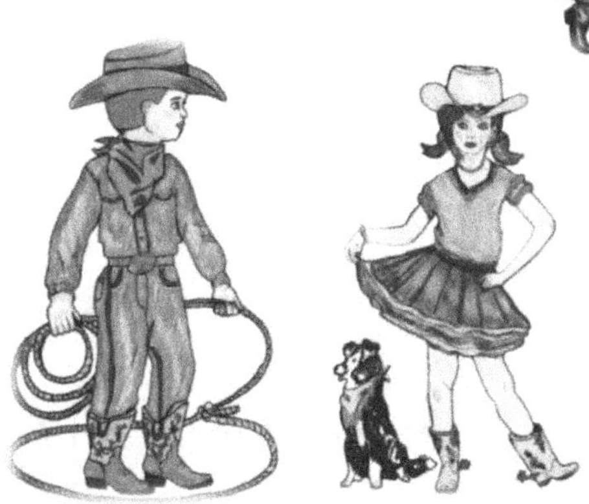

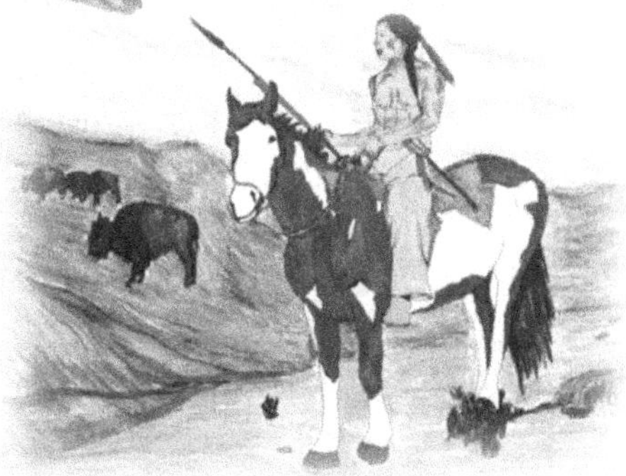

ILLUSTRATED BY: C. JUDIE WILLIAMS

Also Available from
Dancing In The Light

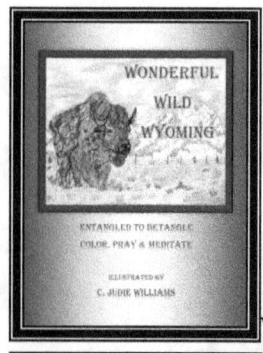 Wonderful Wild Wyoming: Entangled   ISBN-13: 978-0692549780

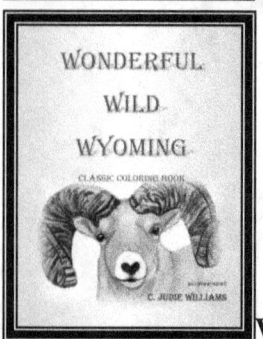 Wonderful Wild Wyoming: Classic   ISBN-13: 978-0692570487

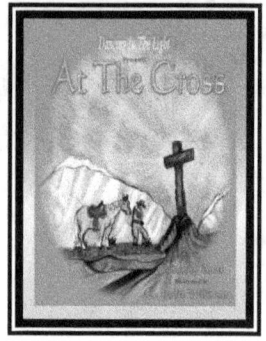 AT The Cross   **ISBN-10: 0692669760**

Contact Information
C. Judie Williams
P.O. Box 1983
Riverton, WY 82501
*Email: **Boyd1880@dishmail.net***
Website: Dancinginthelight.co
Phone: (307) 856-6192
Copyright © 2016 Carrie Judie Williams

Dancing In The Light

Wonderful Wild Wyoming's Wild West: Classic Coloring Book

ISBN-13: 978-0692698754
ISBN-10: 0692698752

DEDICATION

For

William "Buzzy" & Jerri Robinson

"for where you go, I will go, and where you lodge, I will lodge. Your people shall be my people, and your God, my God." Ruth 1:16

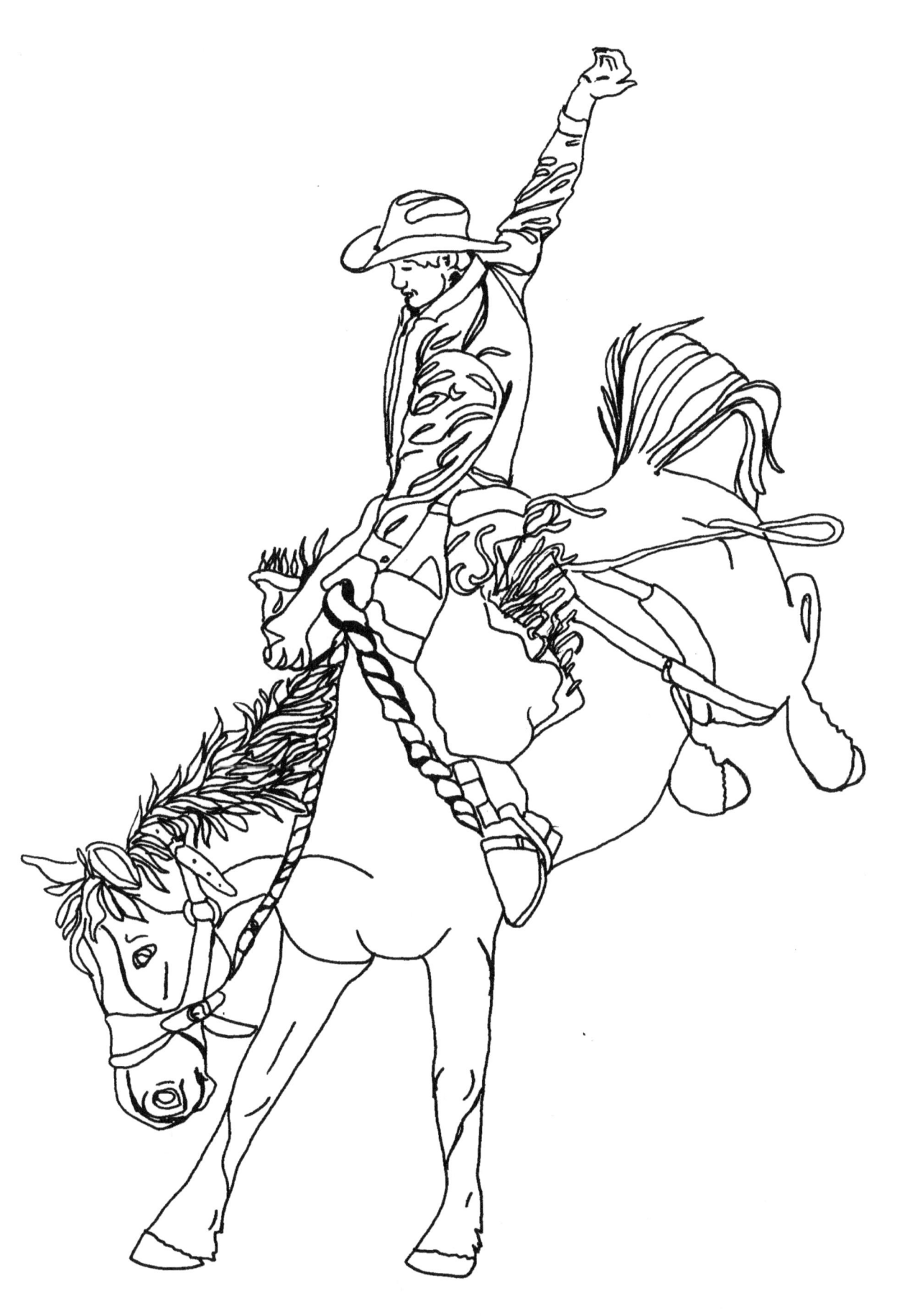

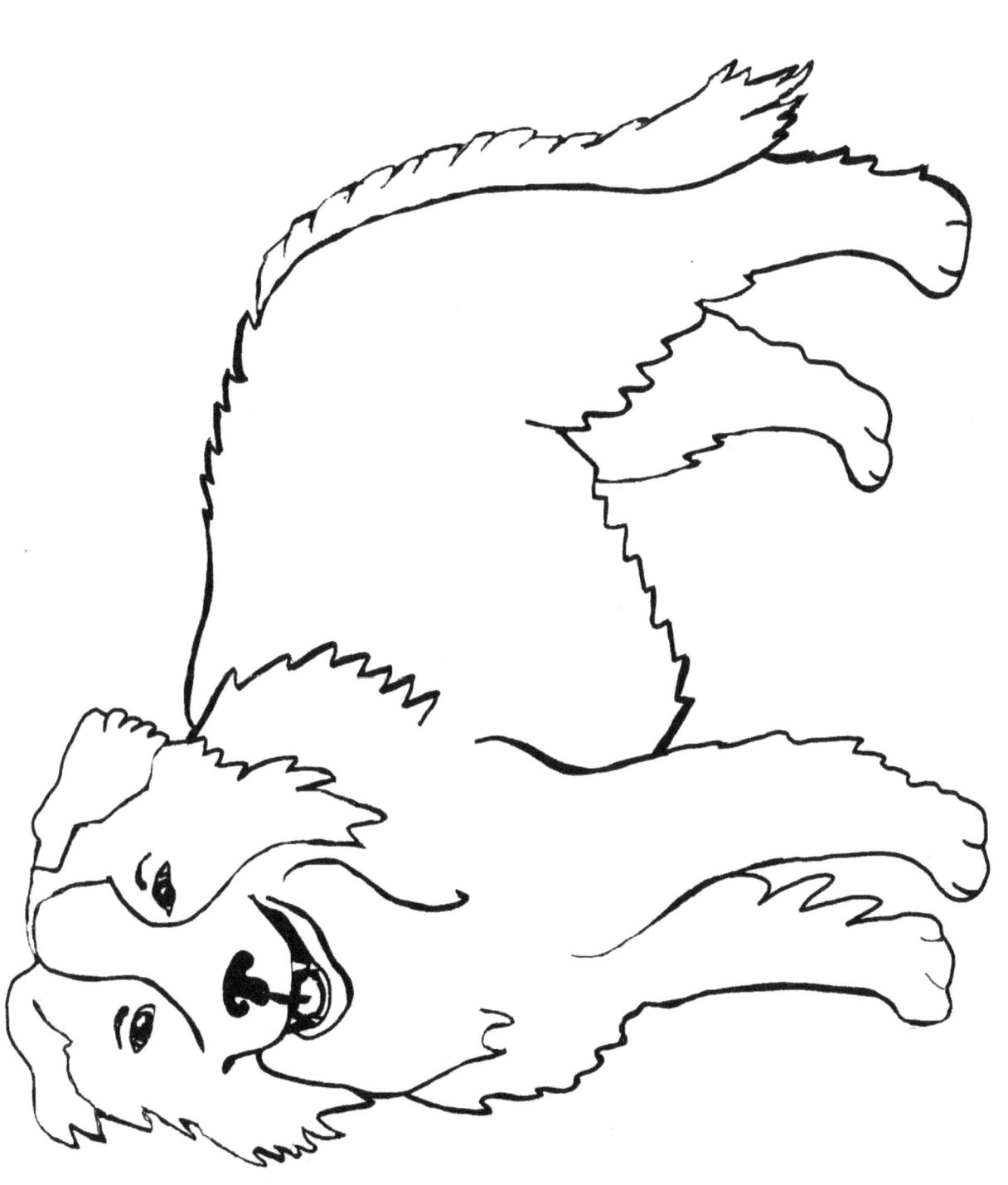

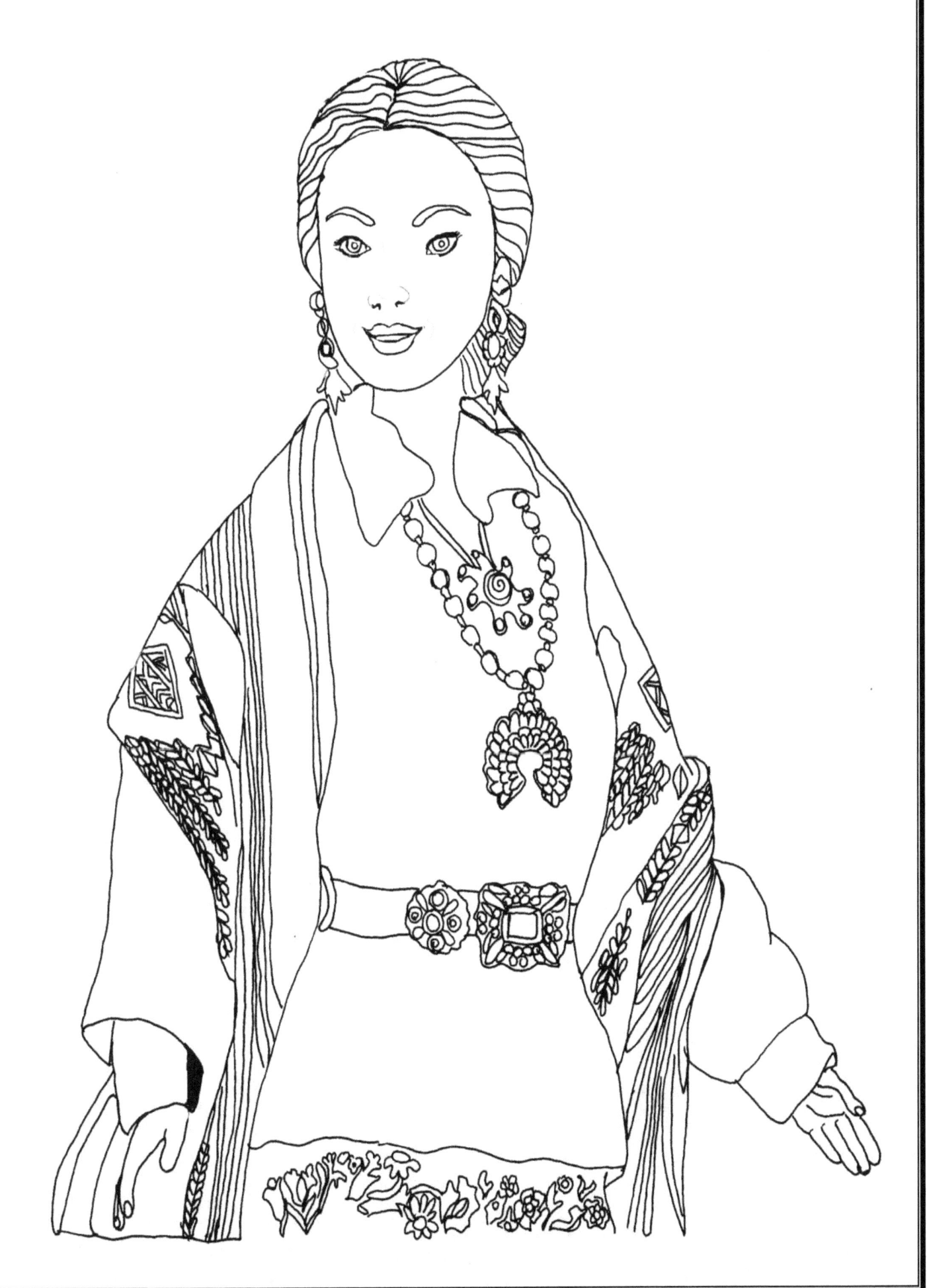

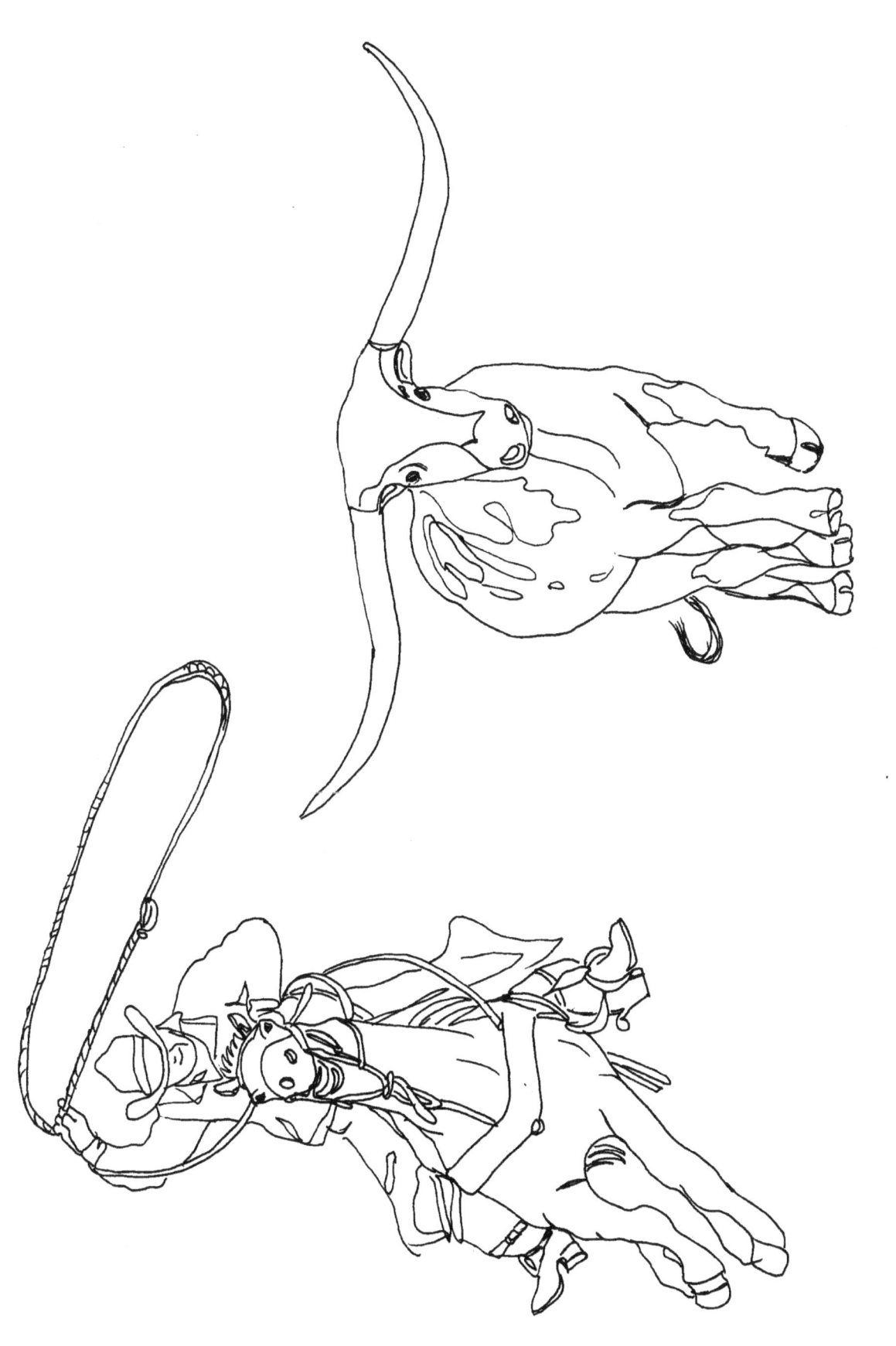

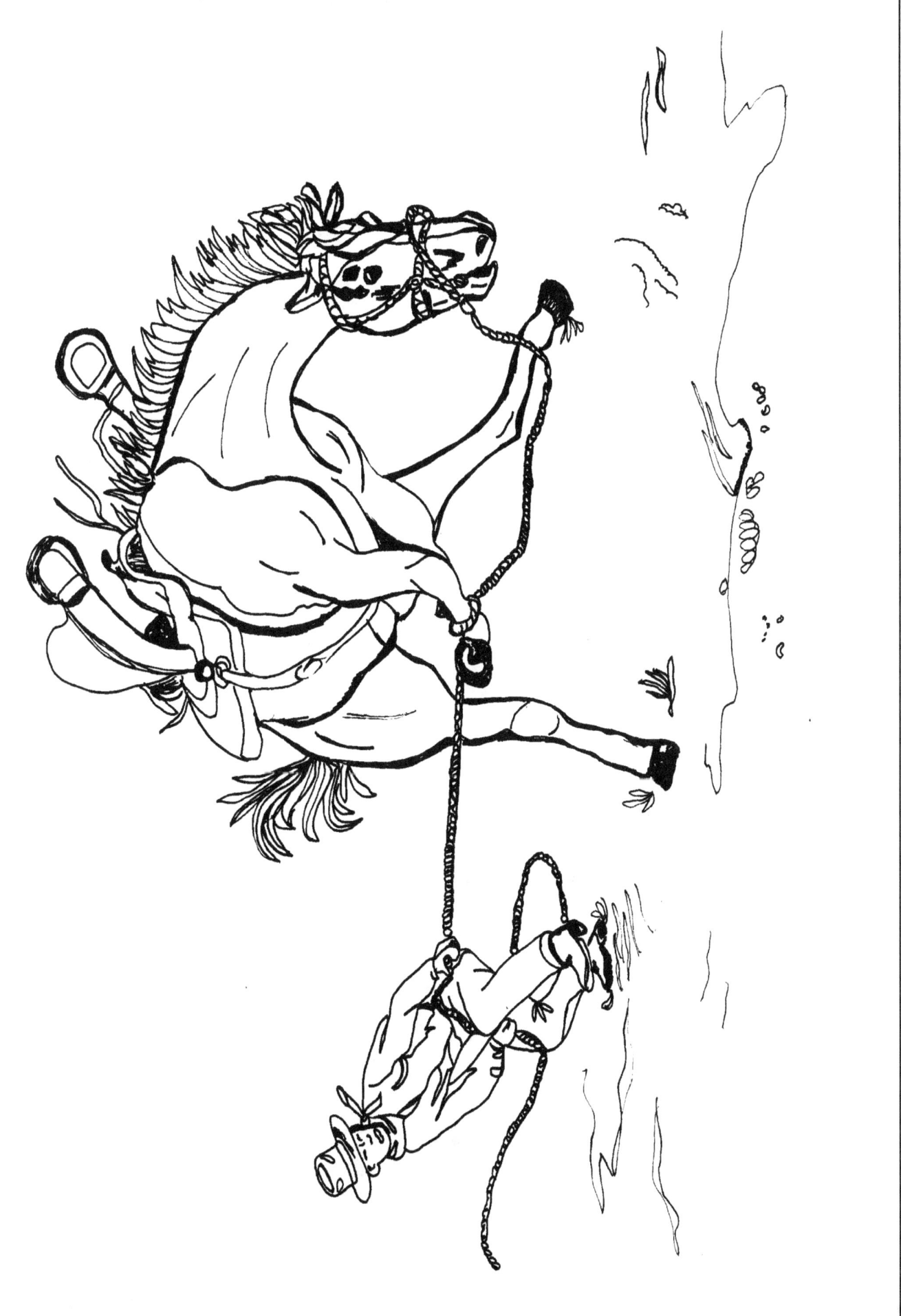

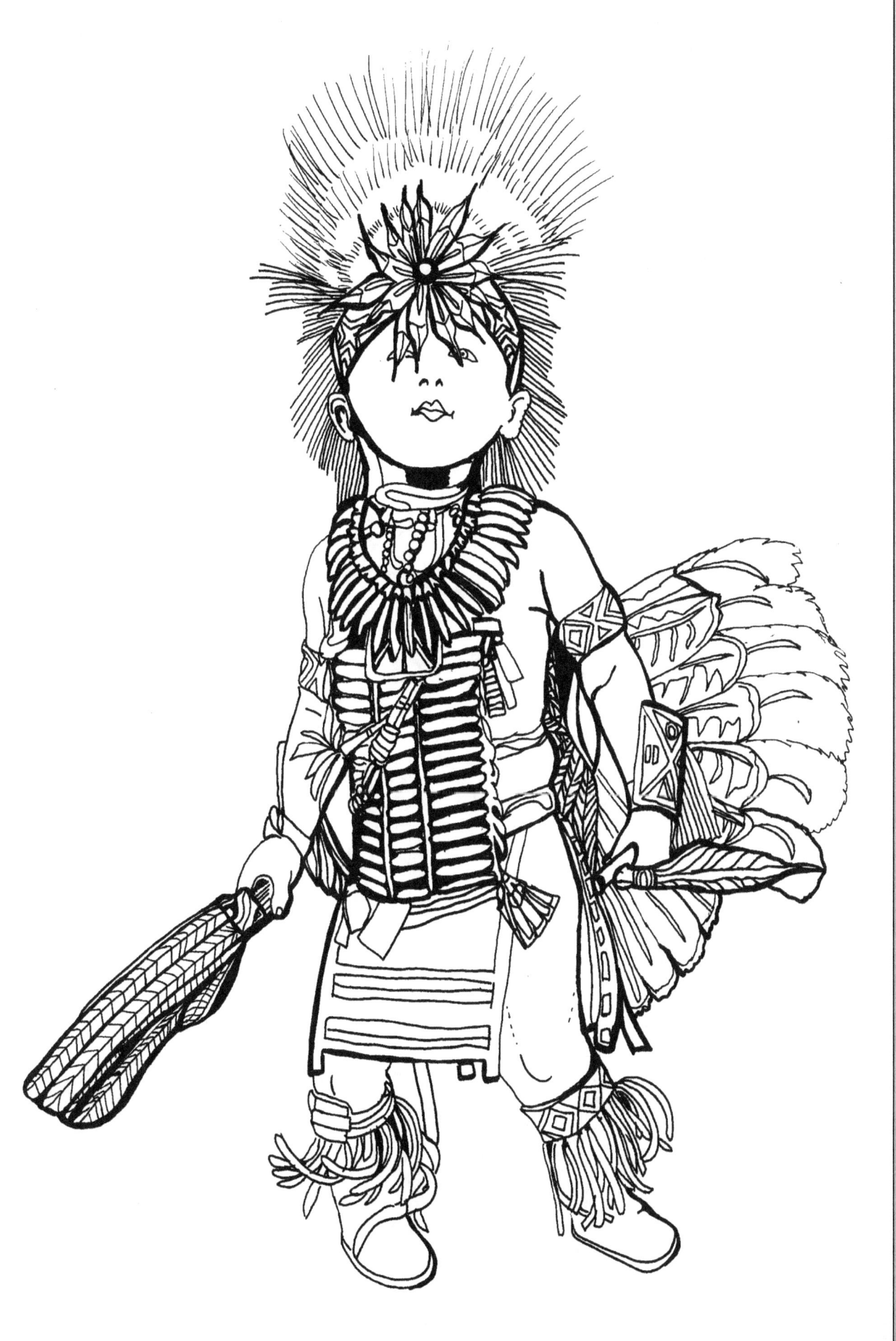

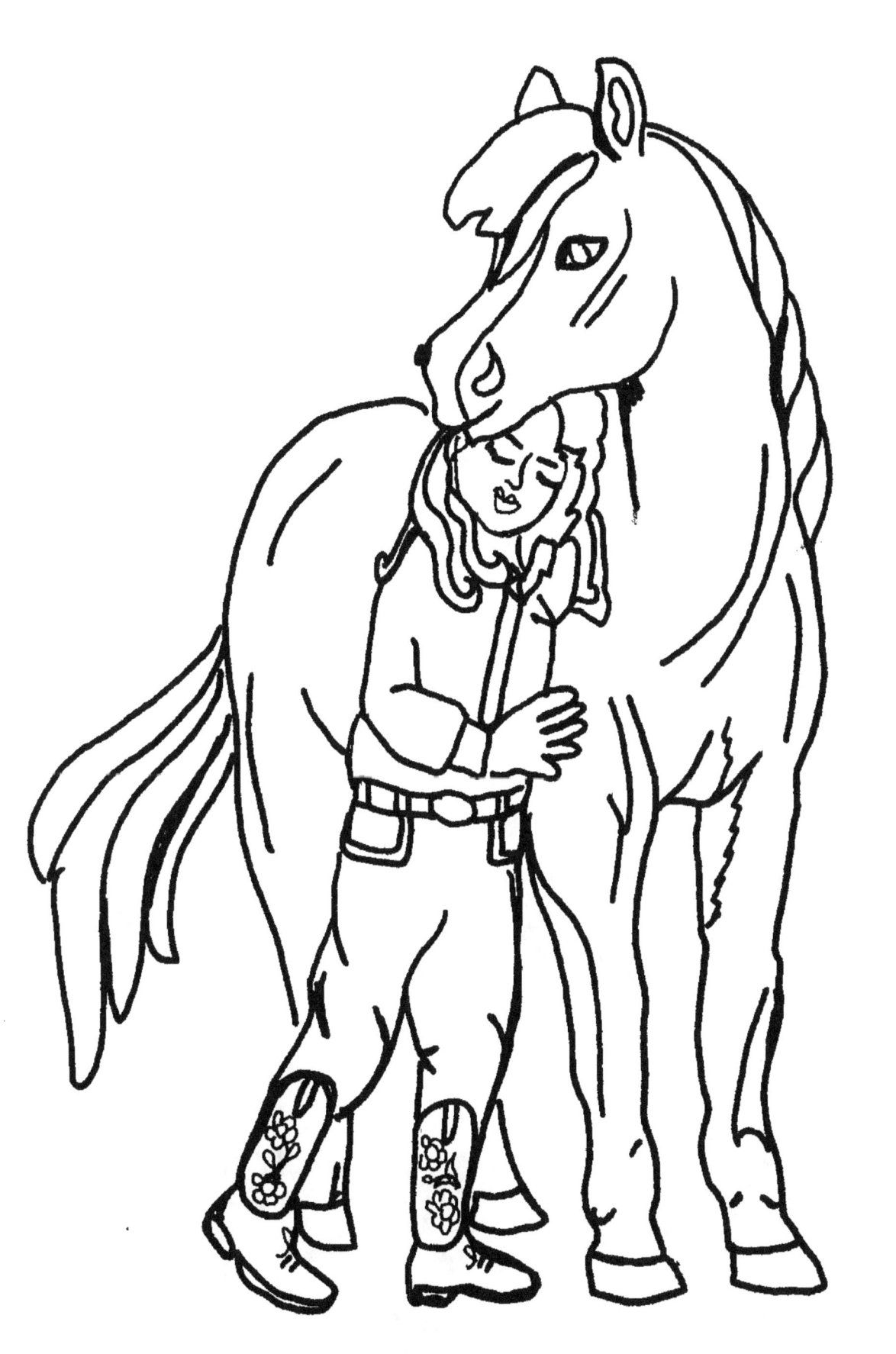

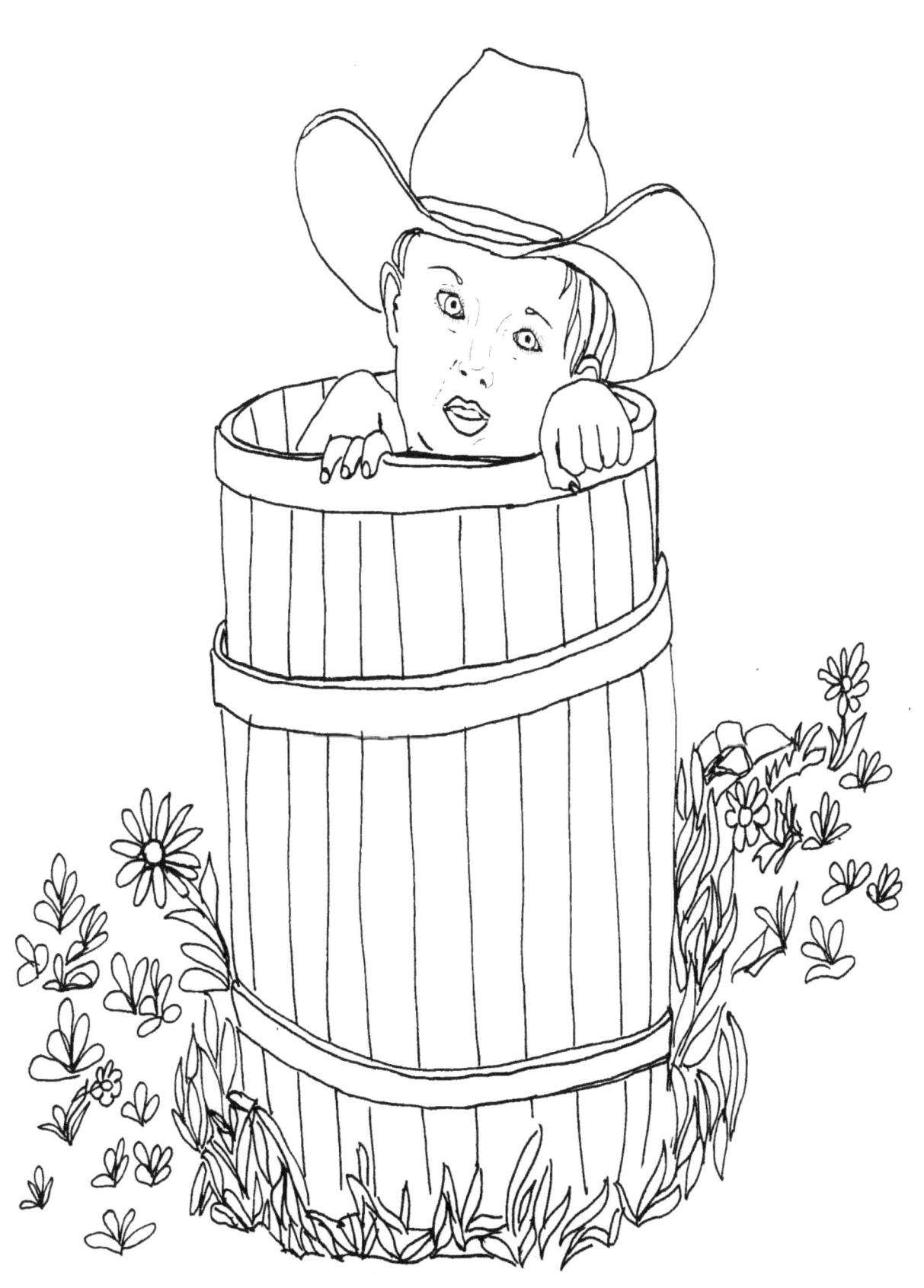

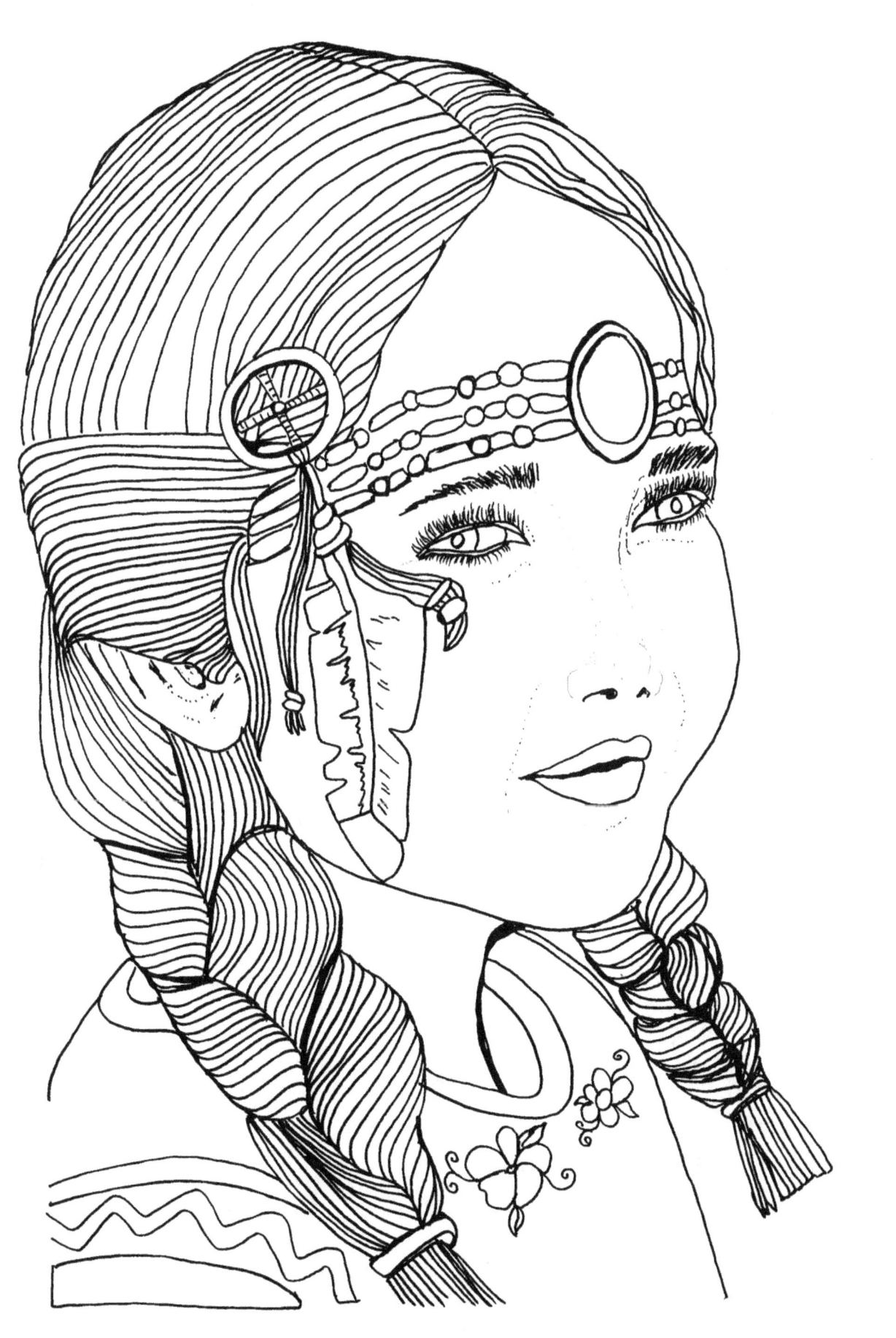

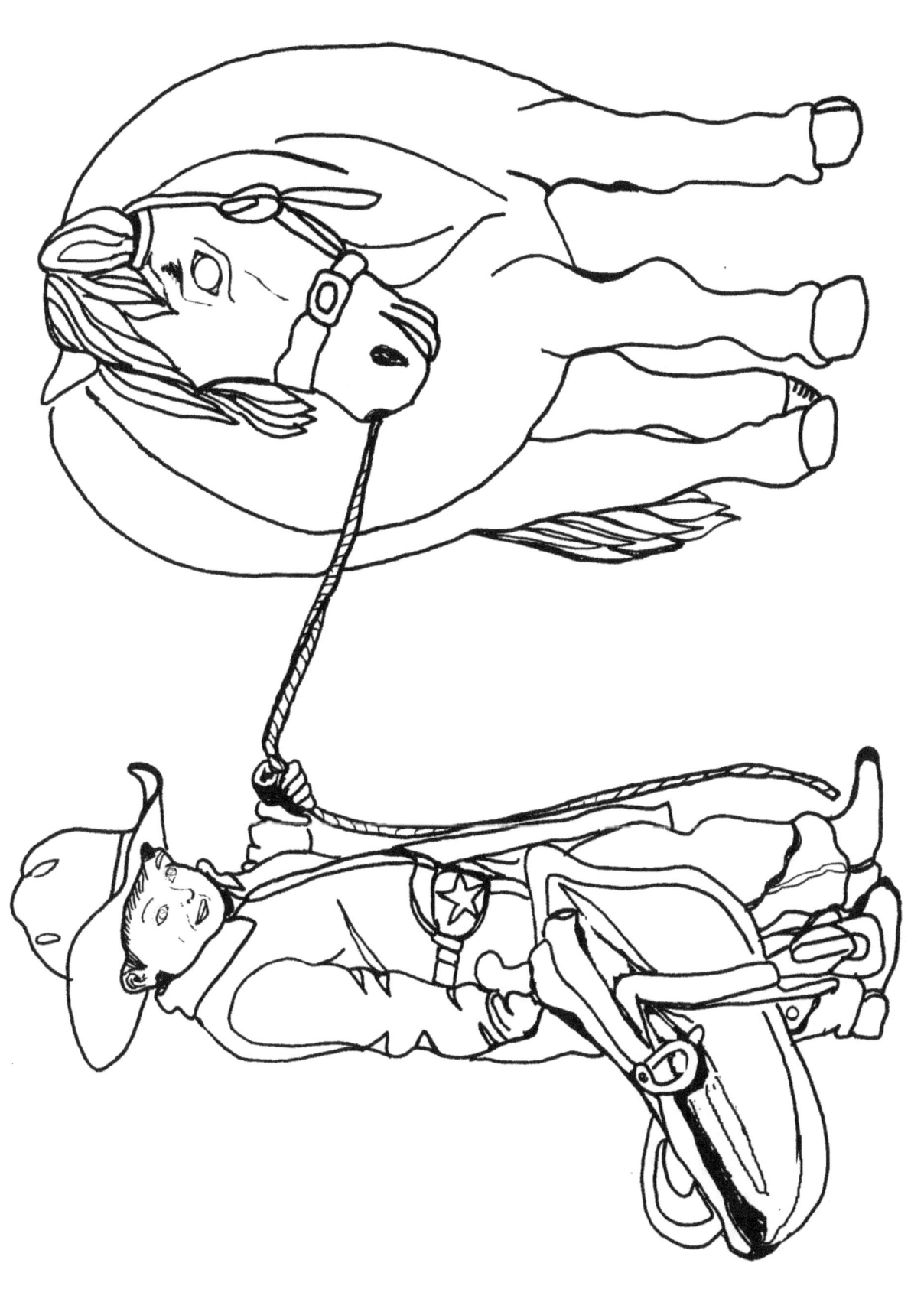

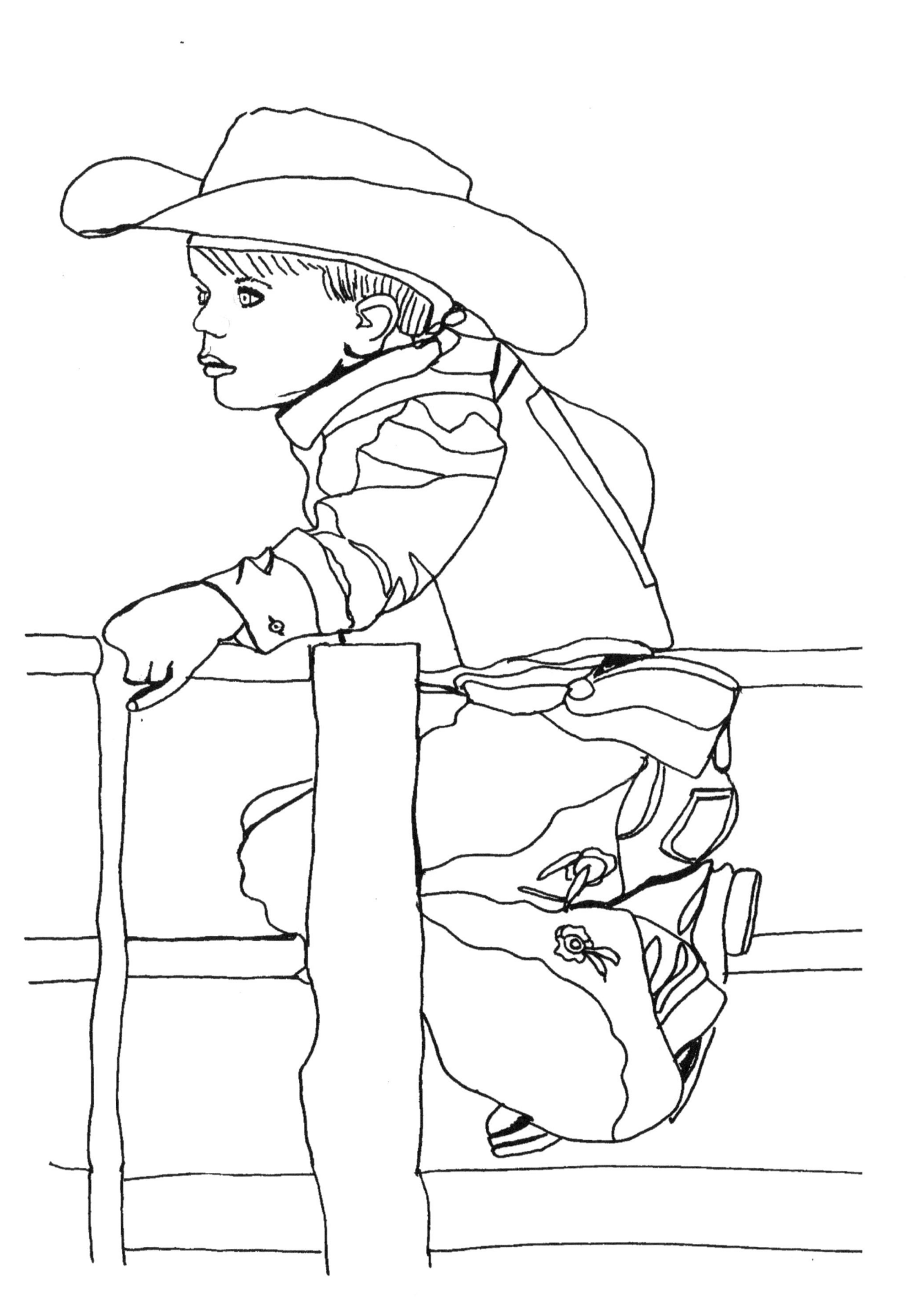

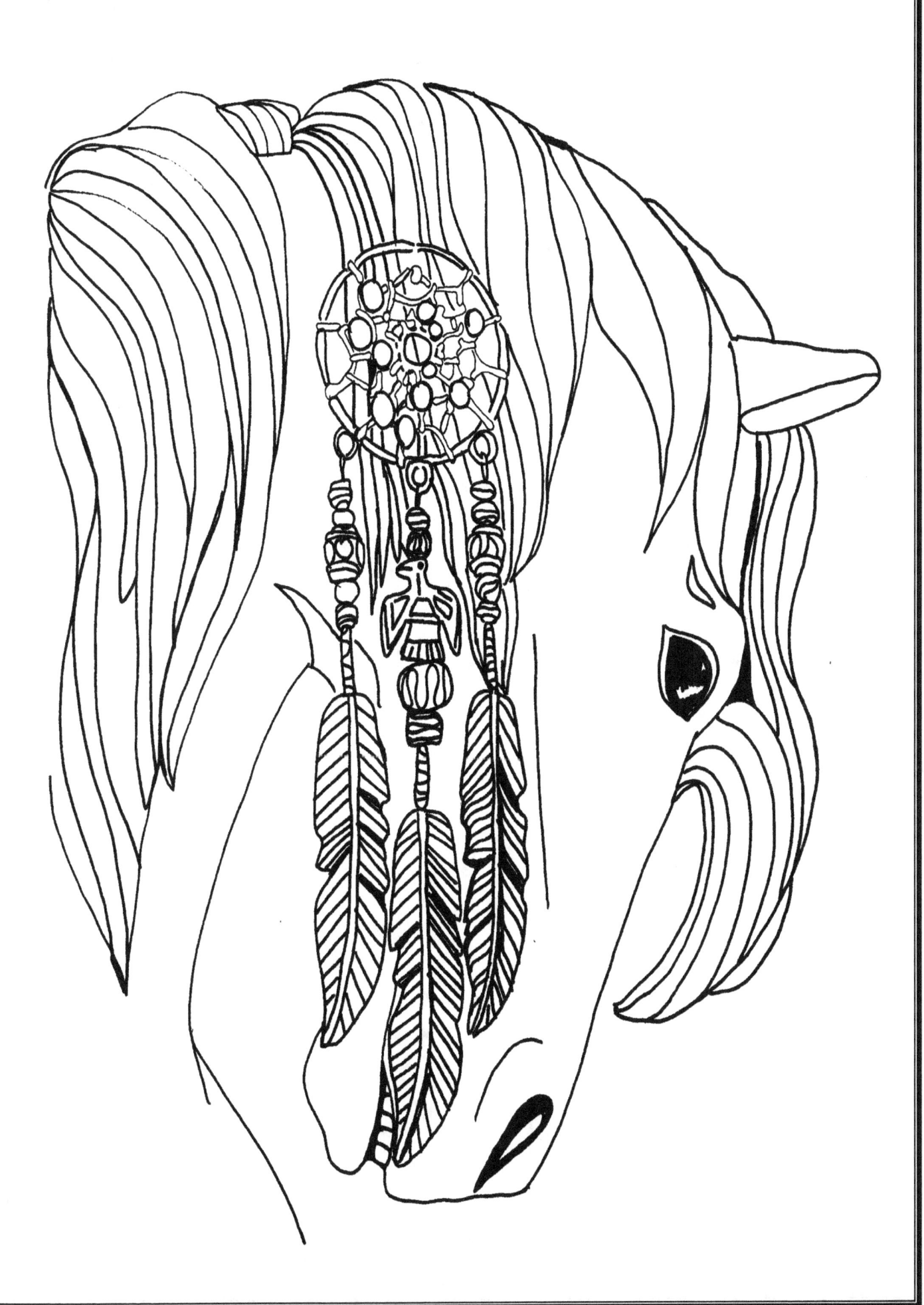

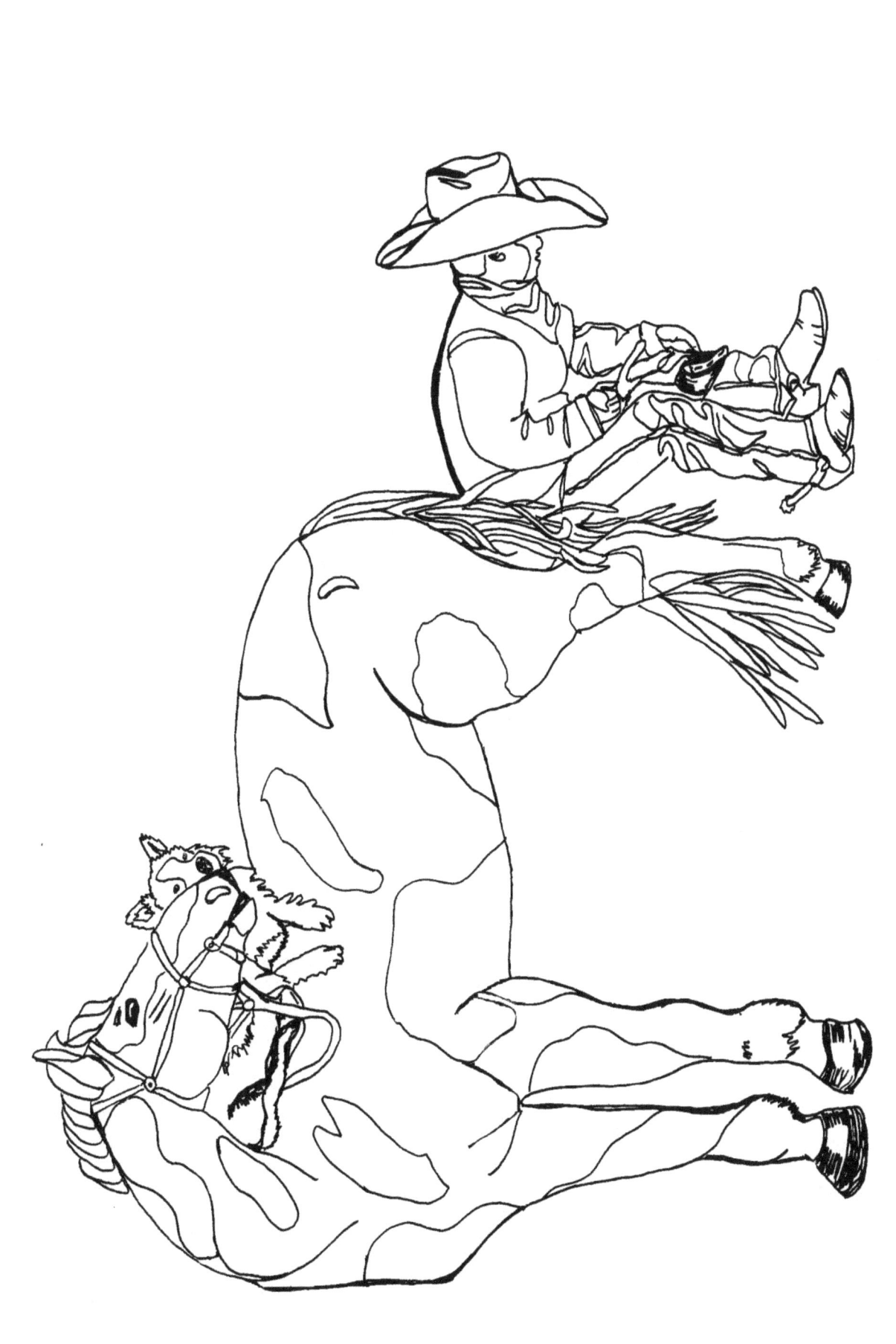

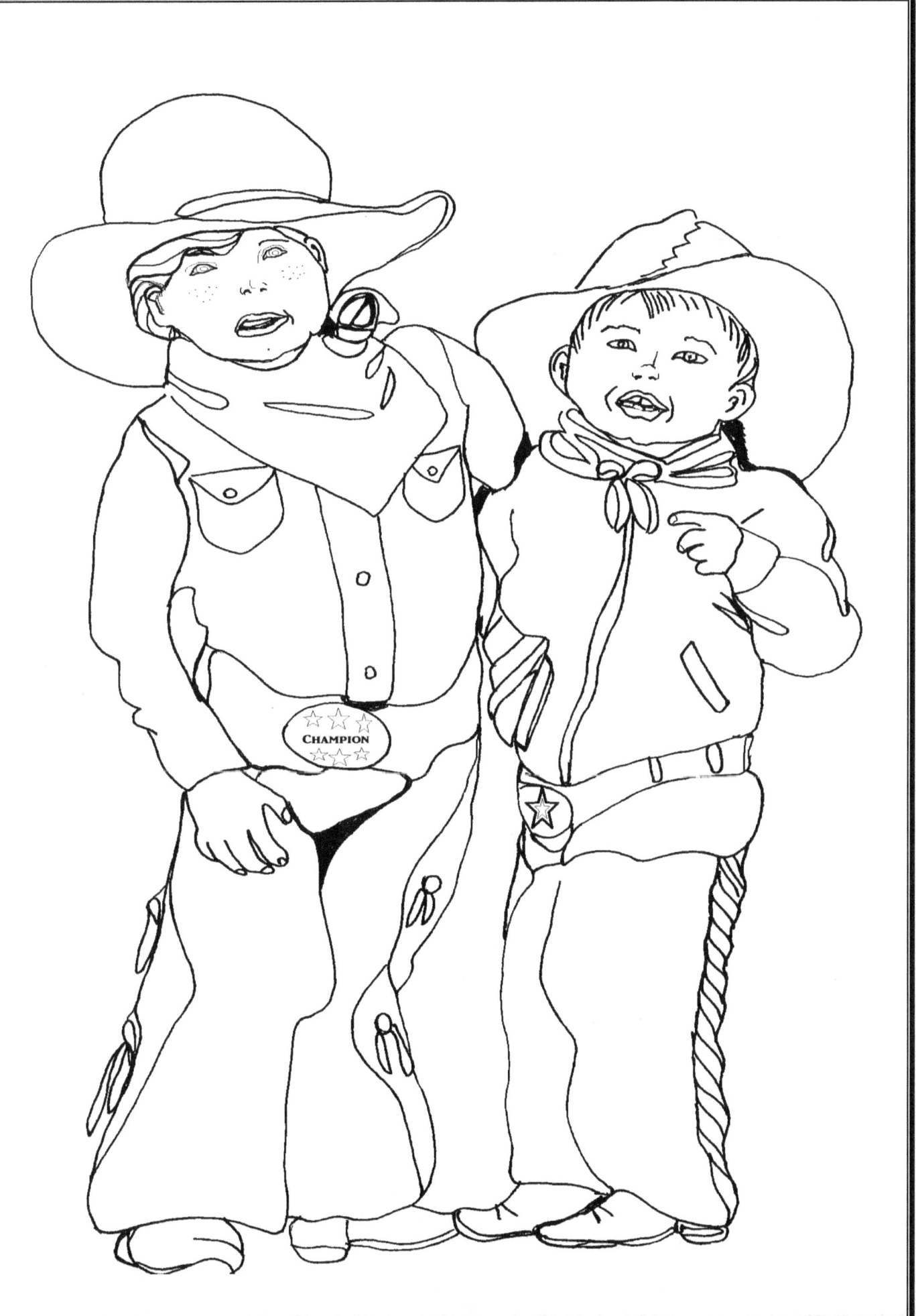

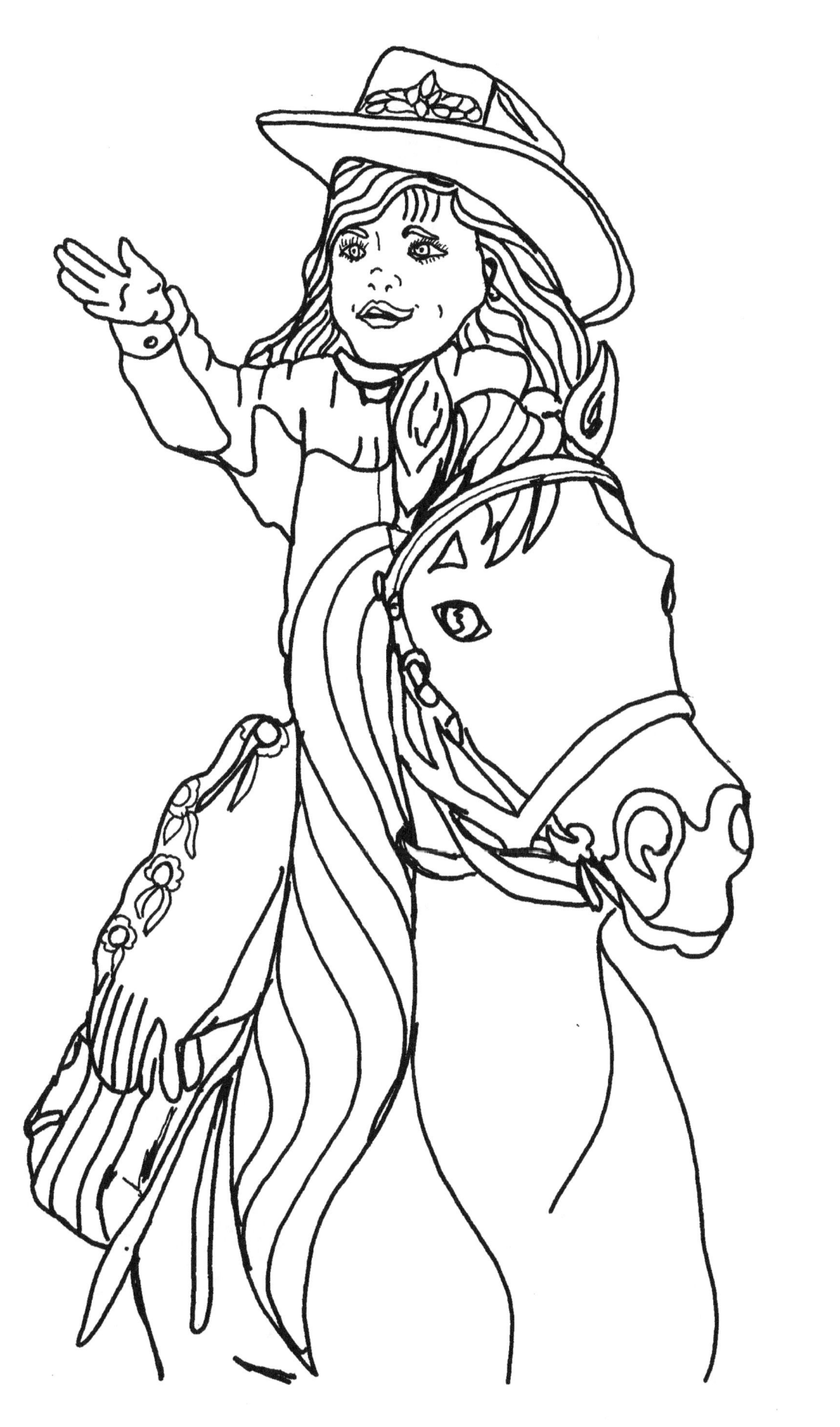

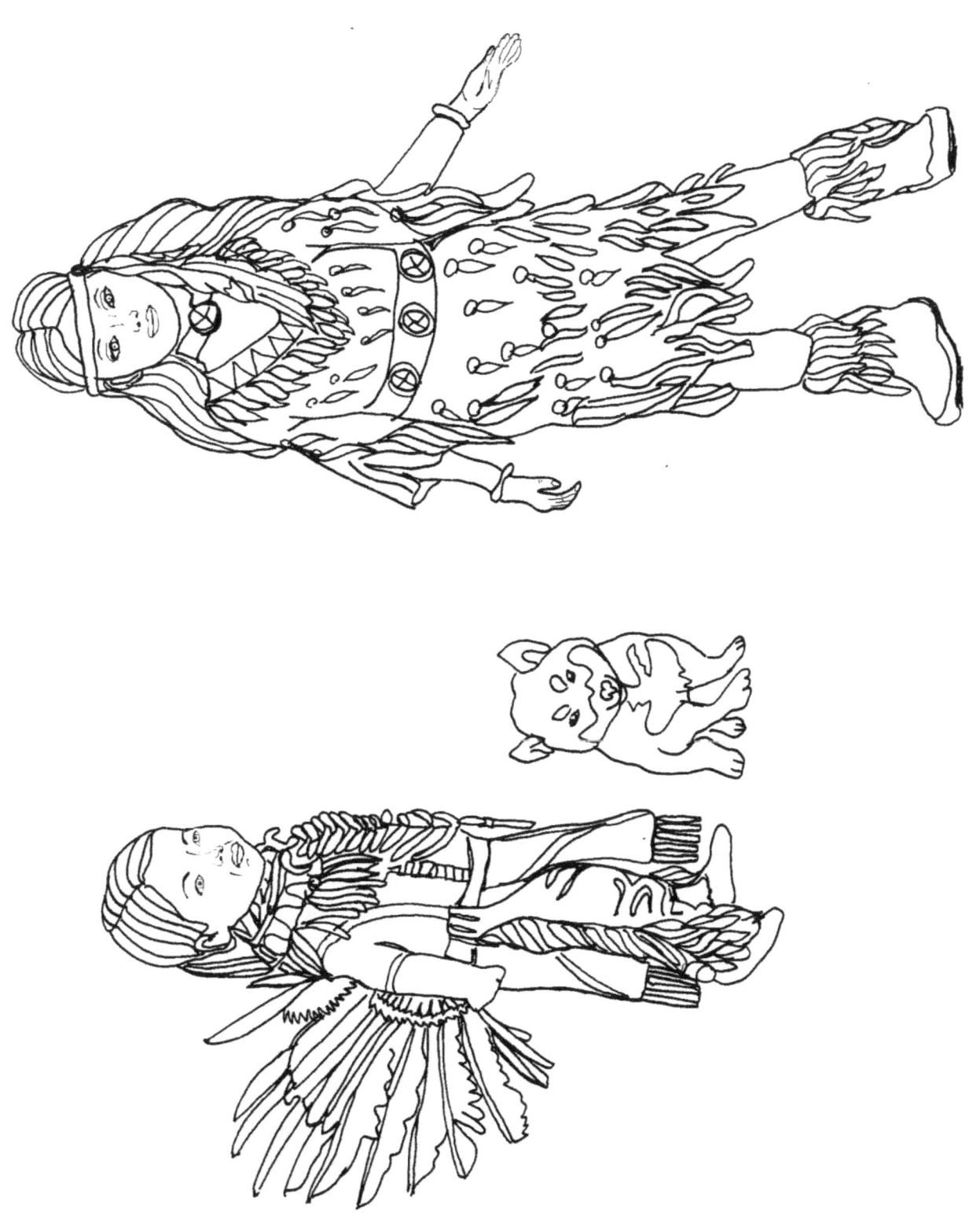

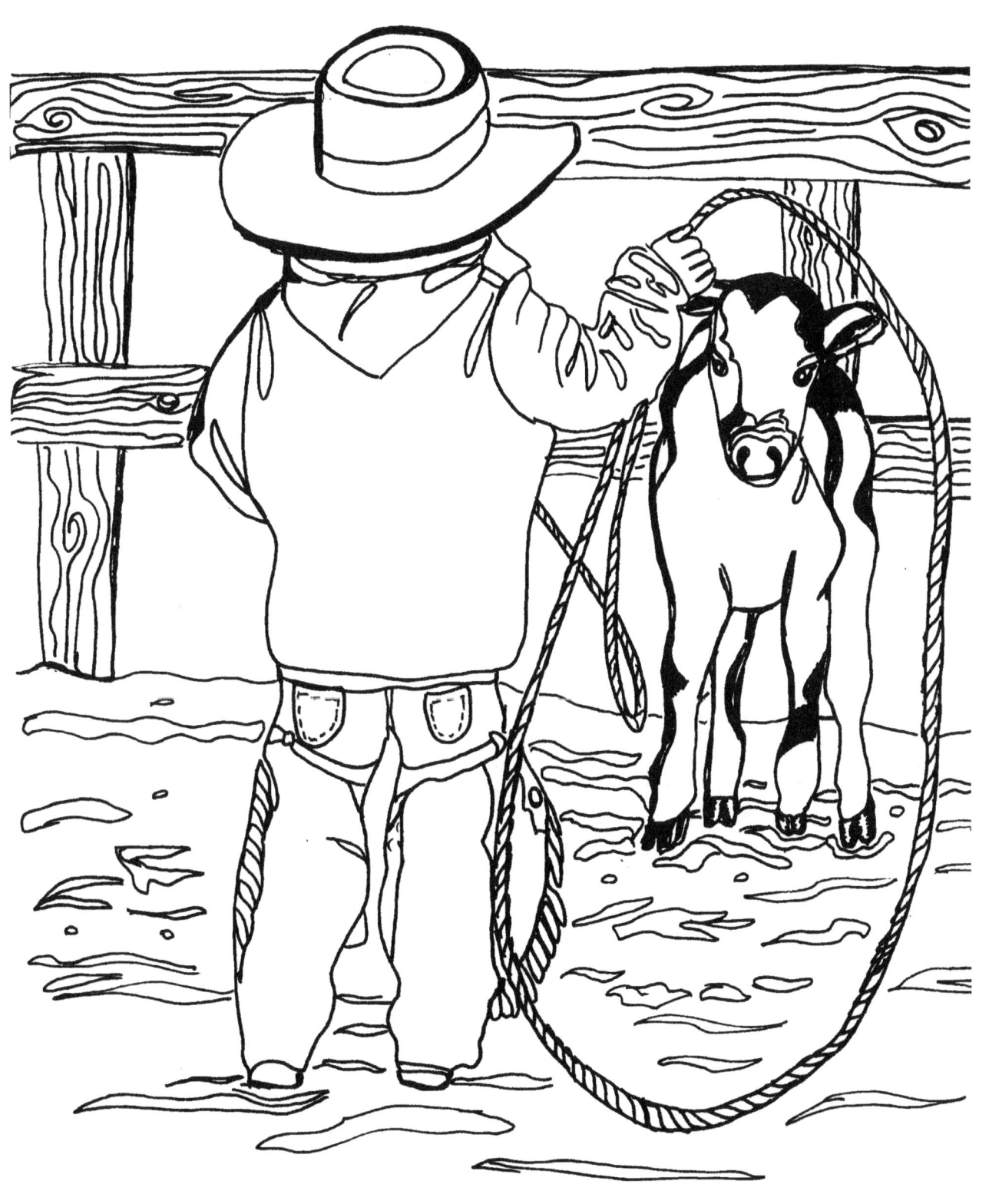

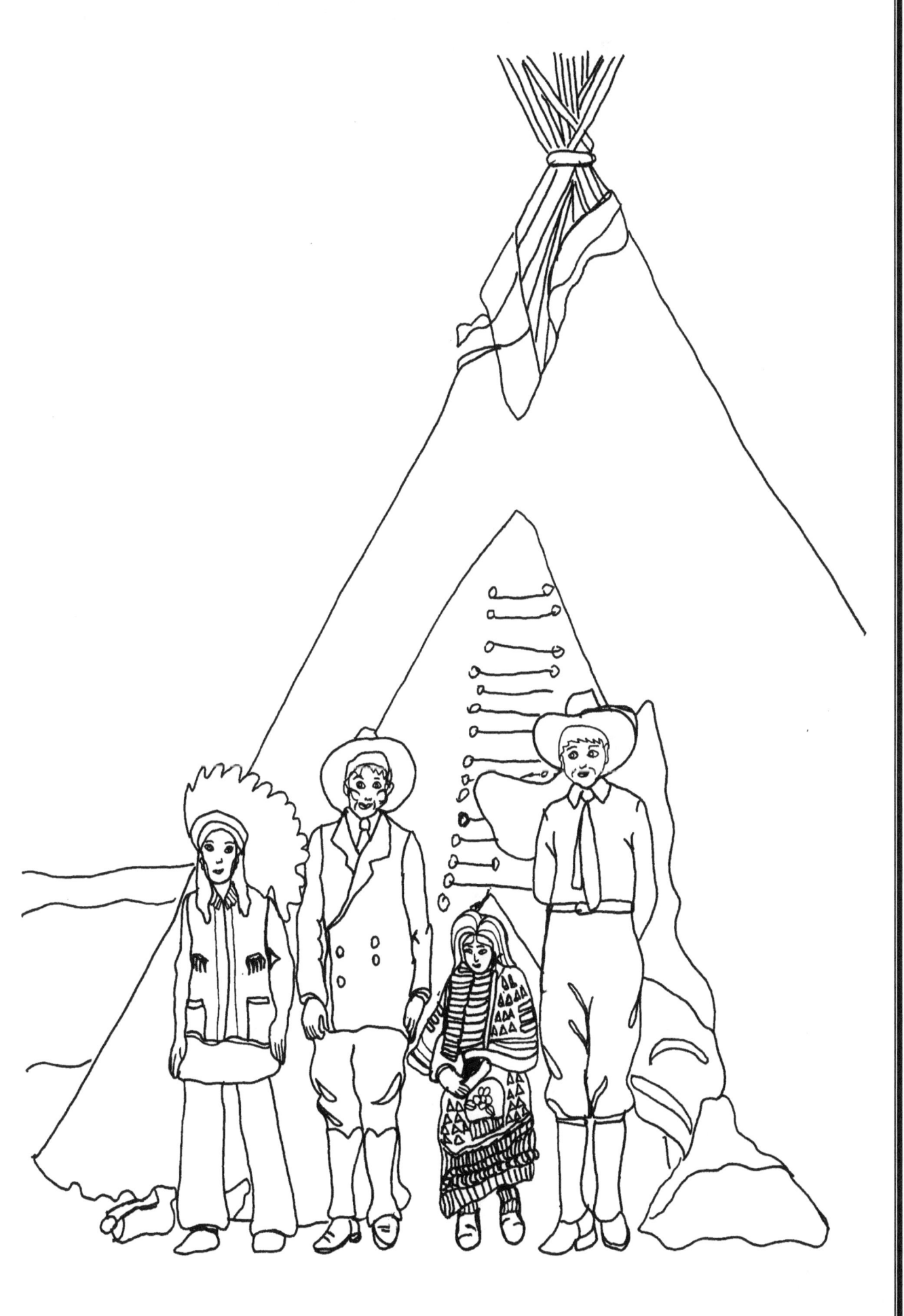

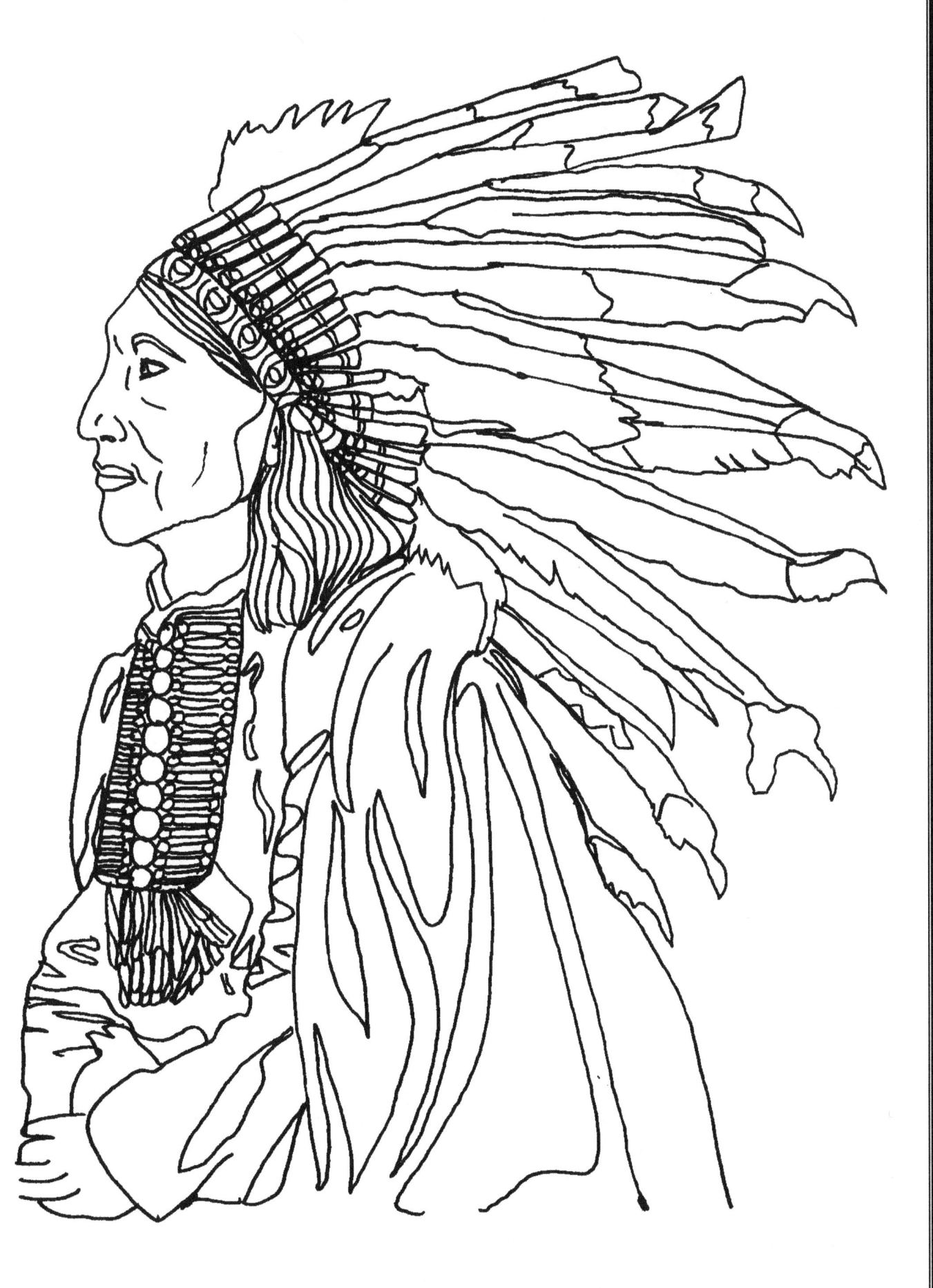

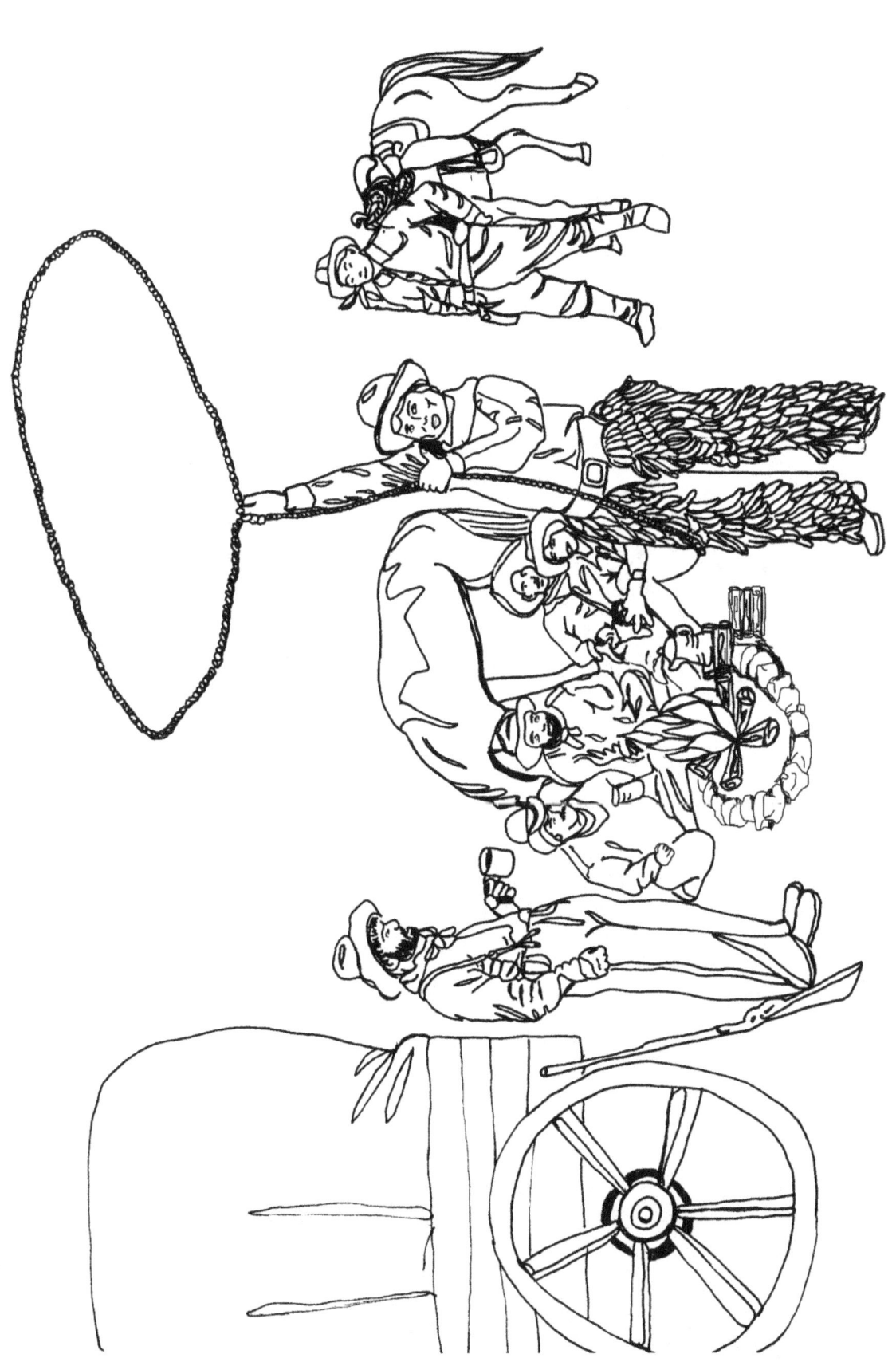

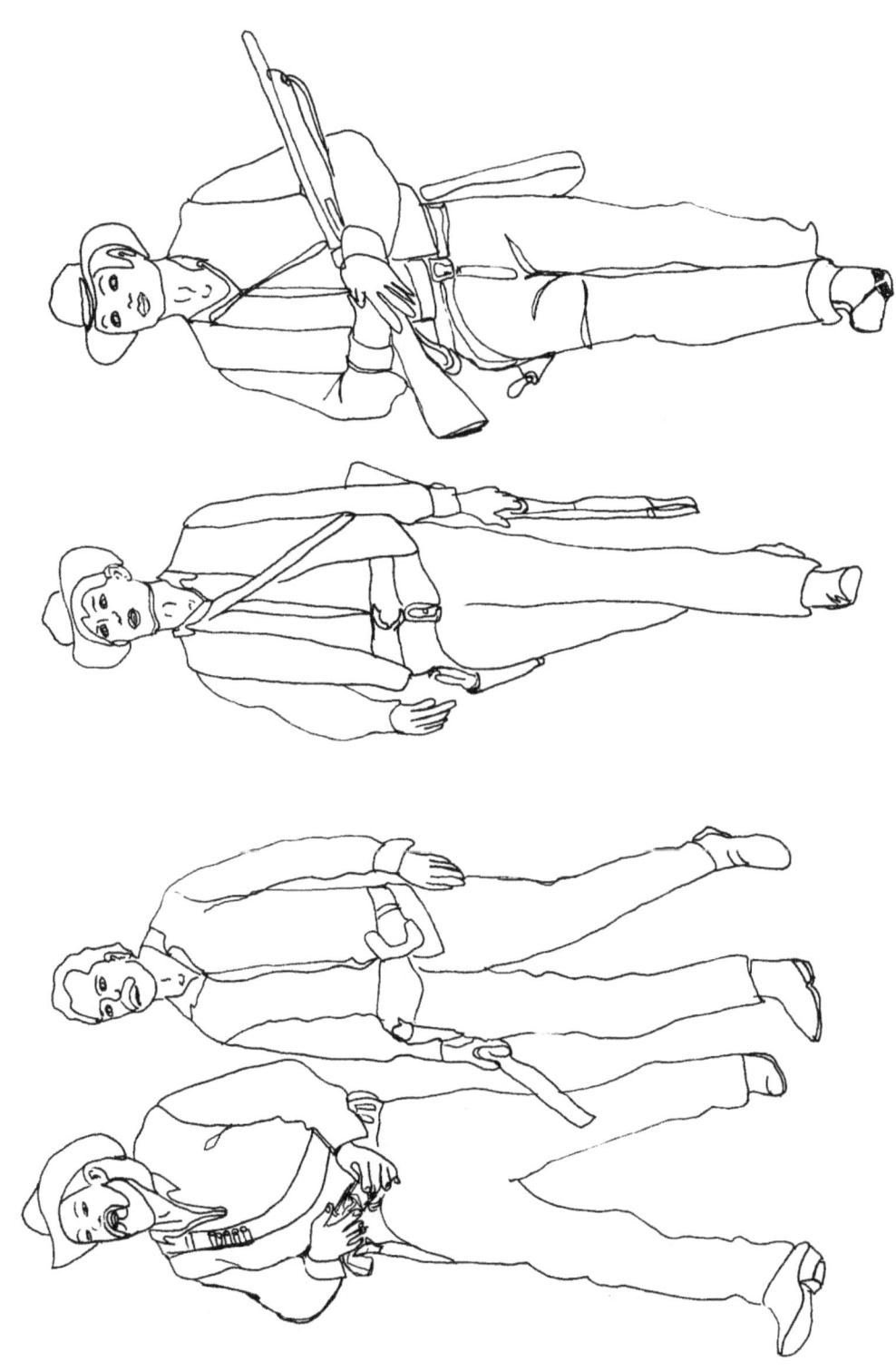

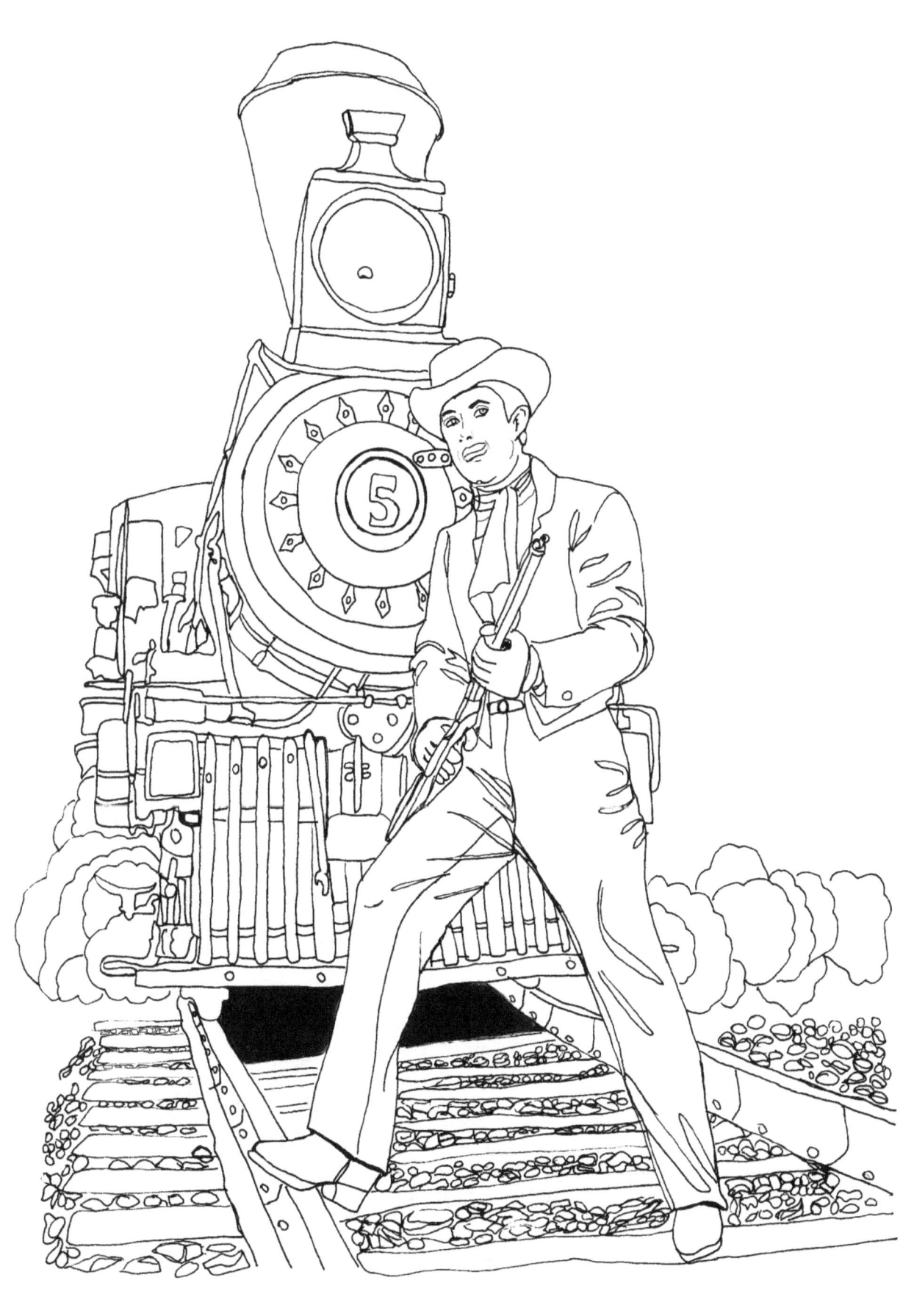

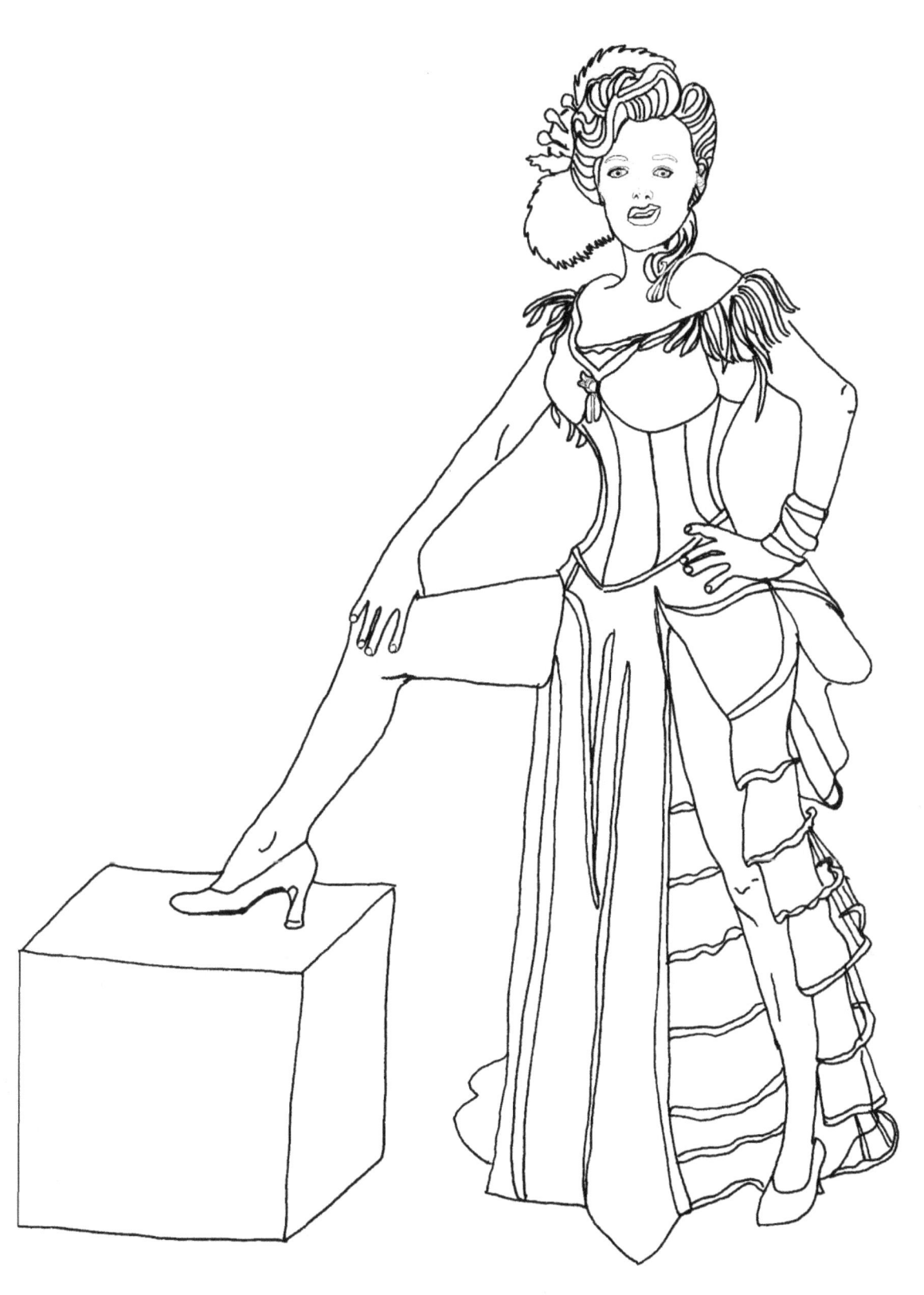

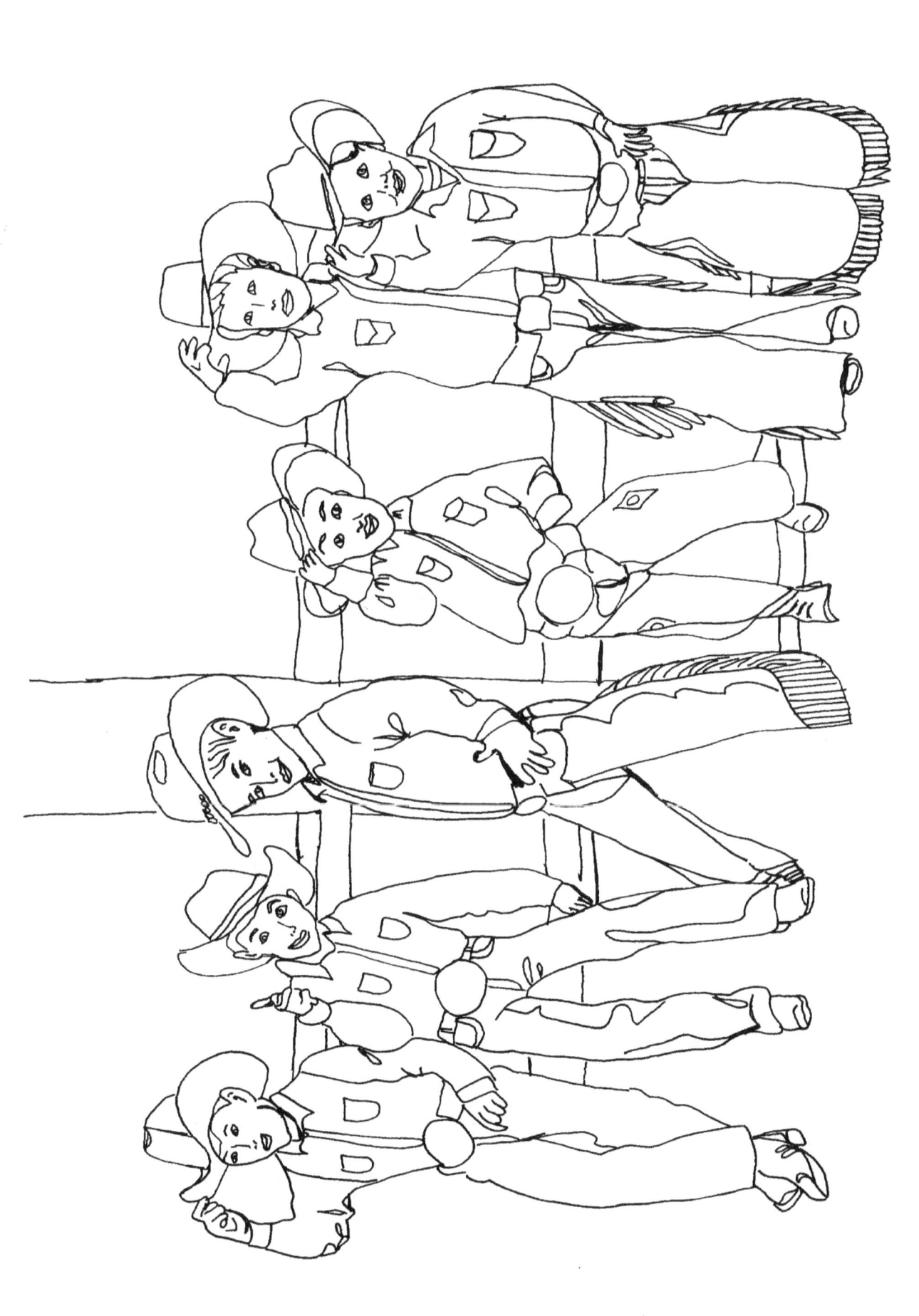

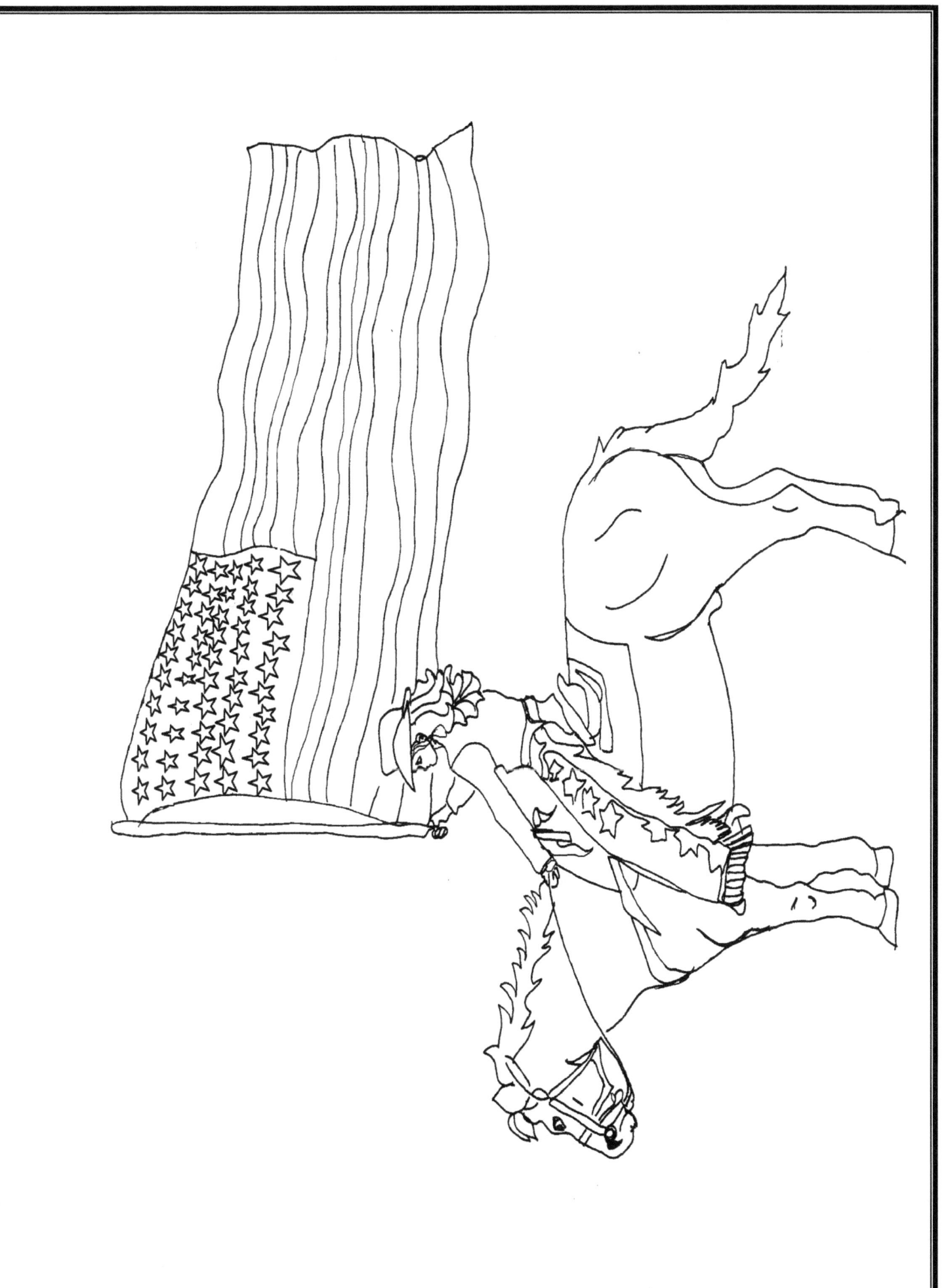

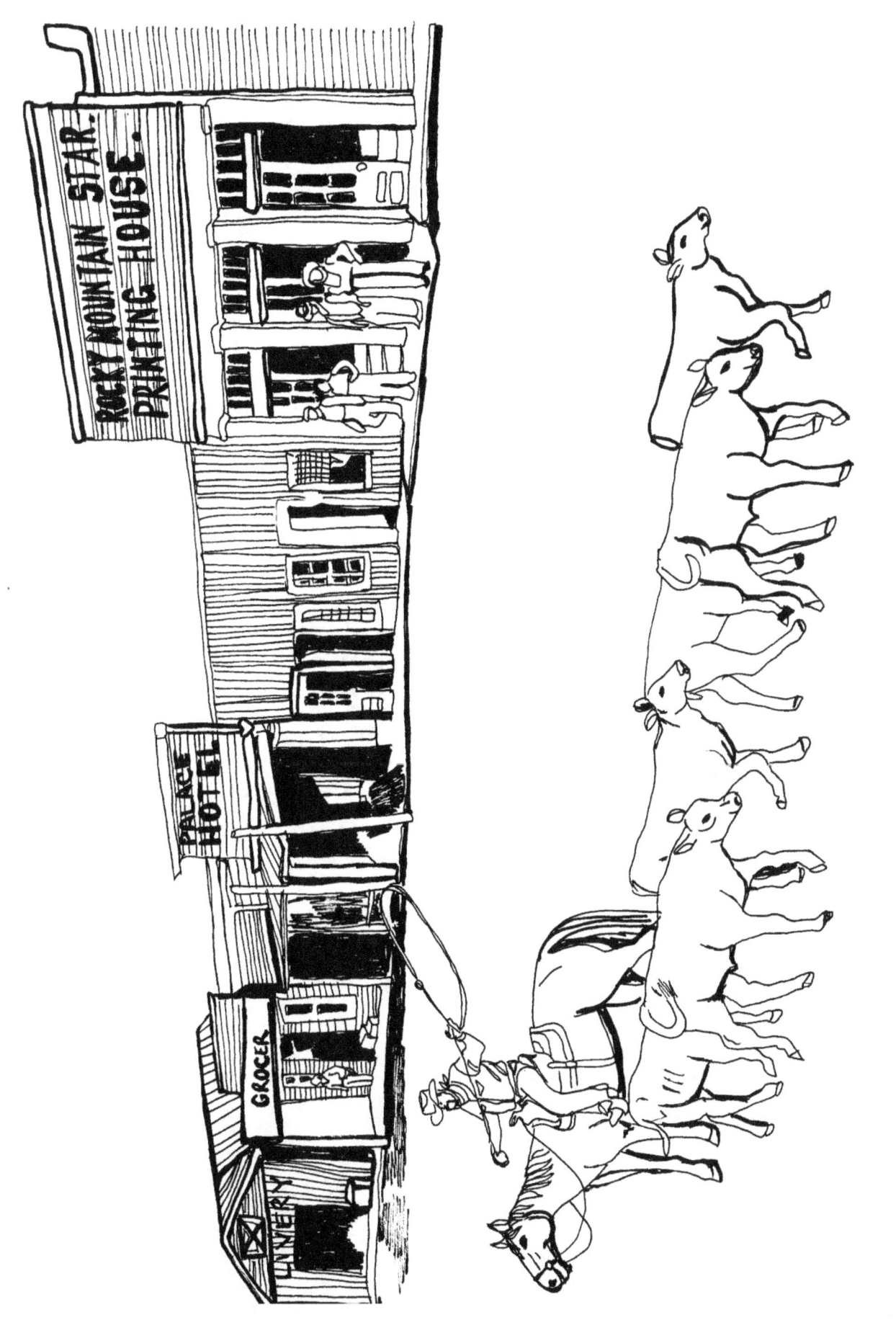

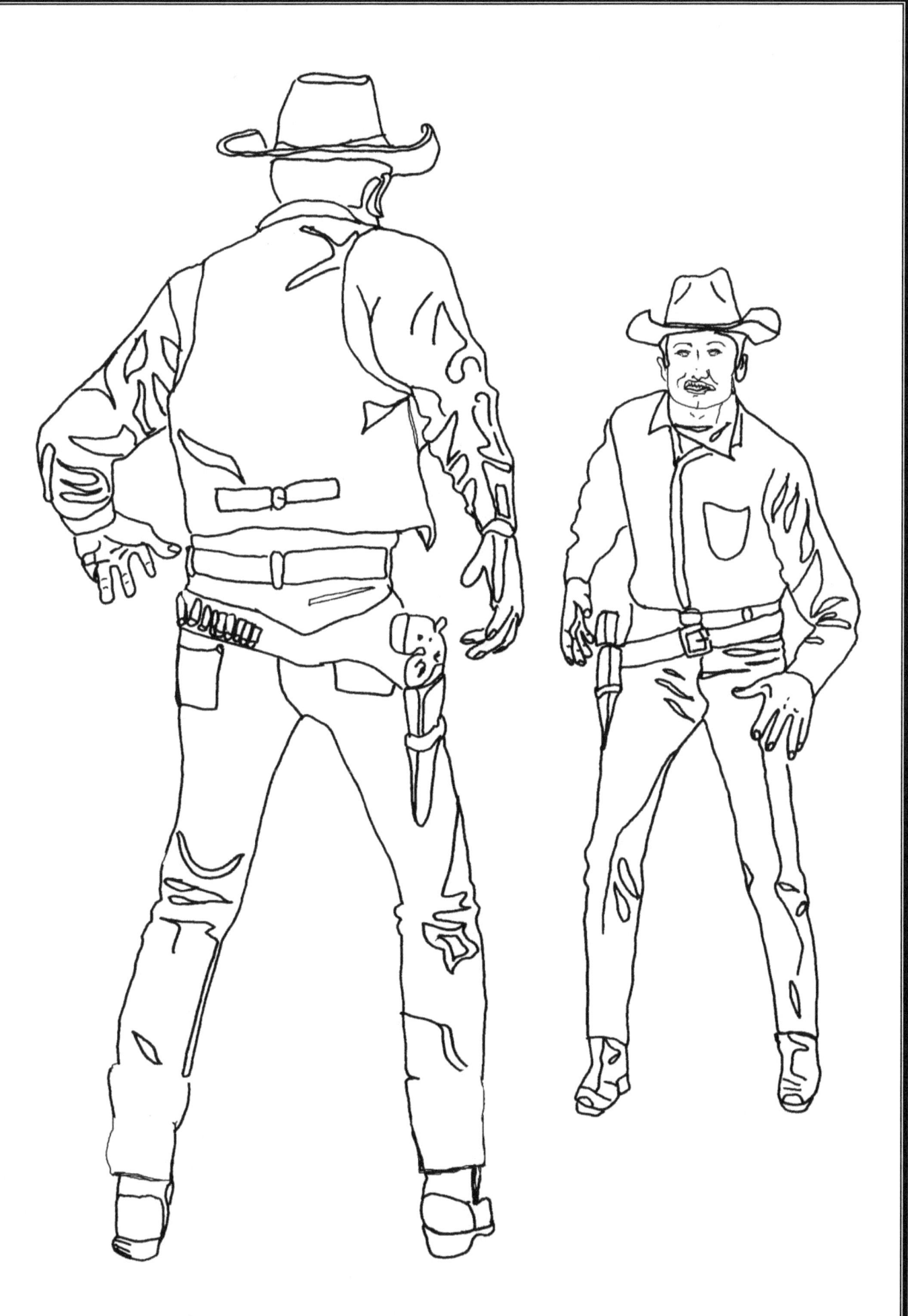

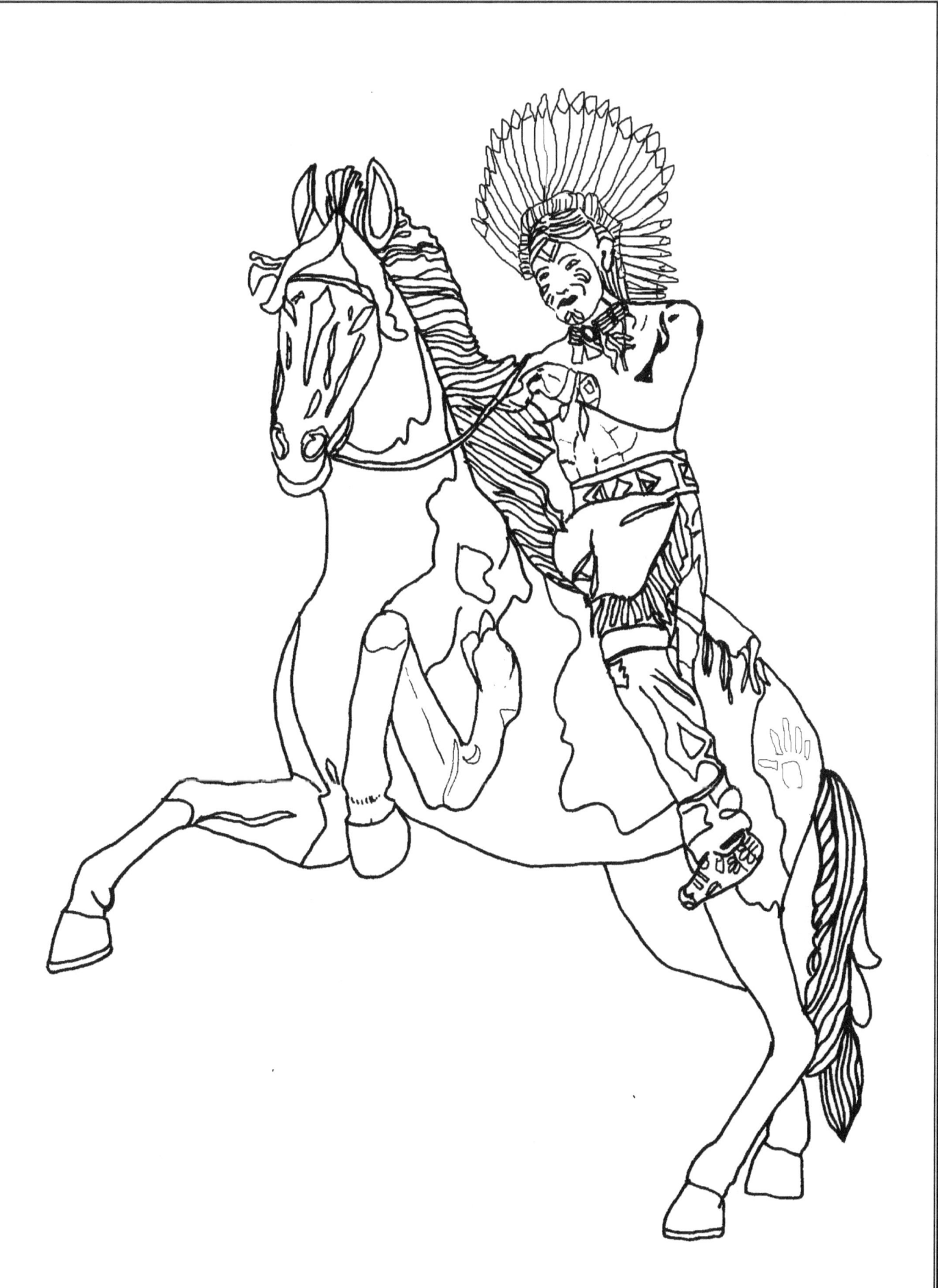

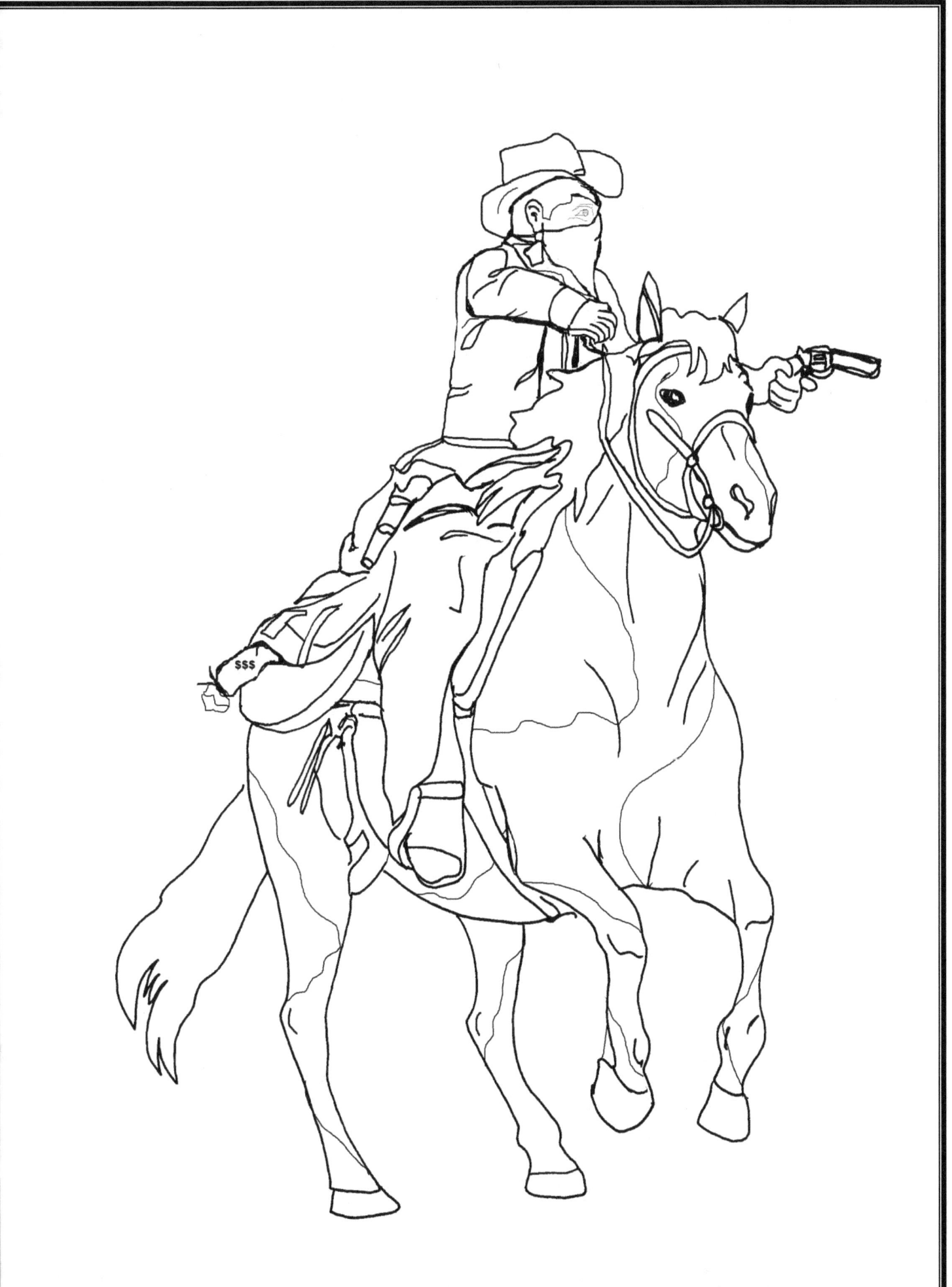

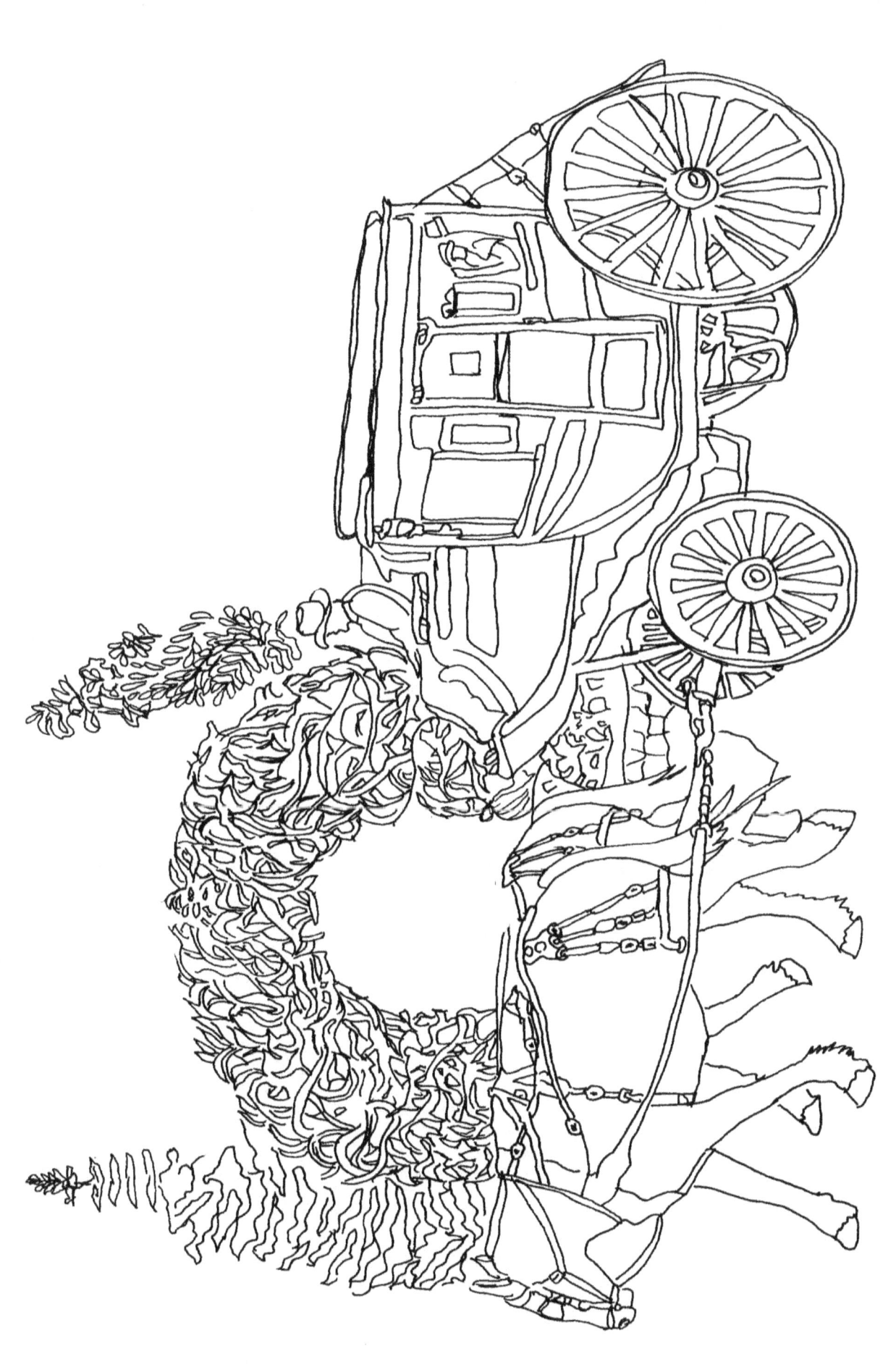

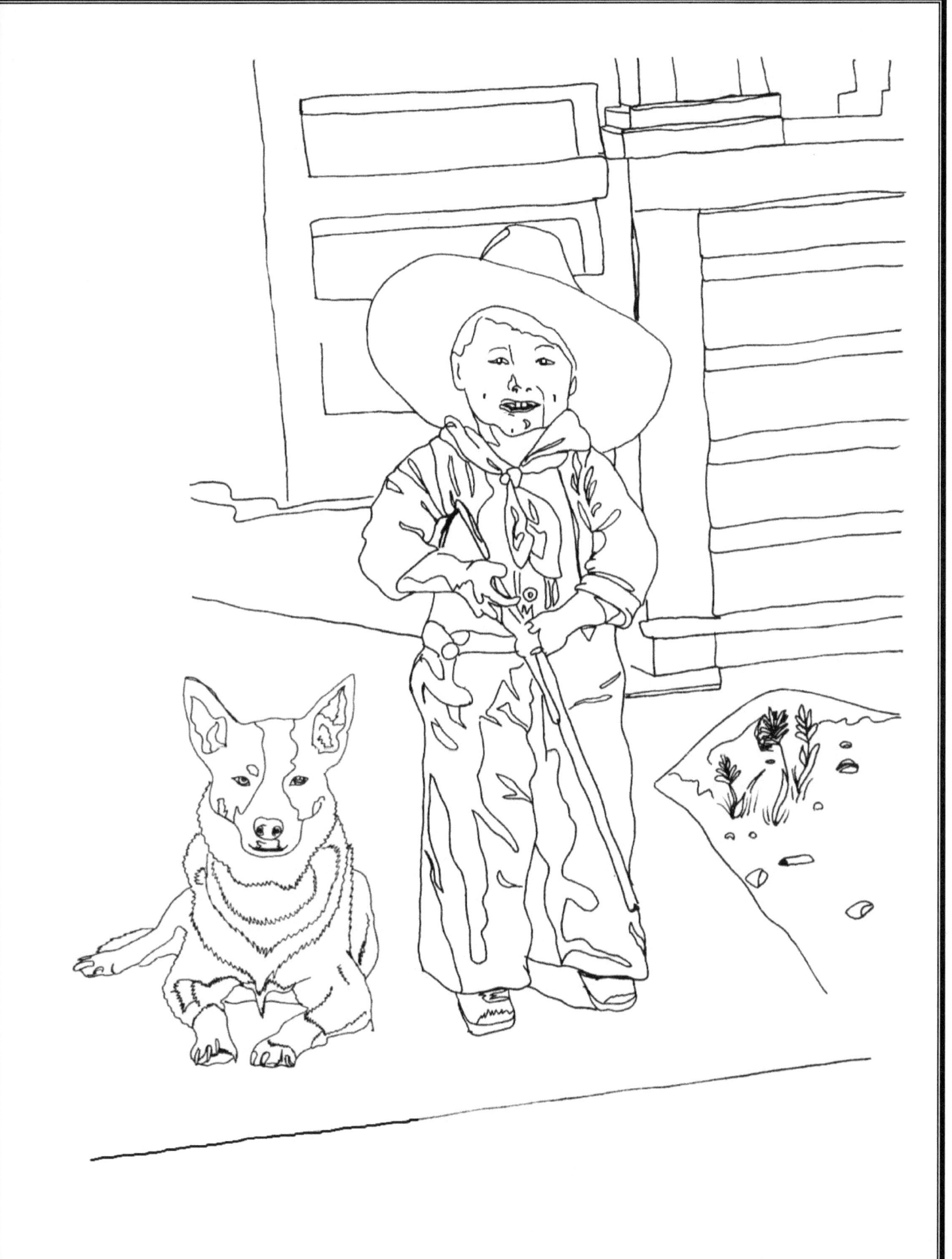

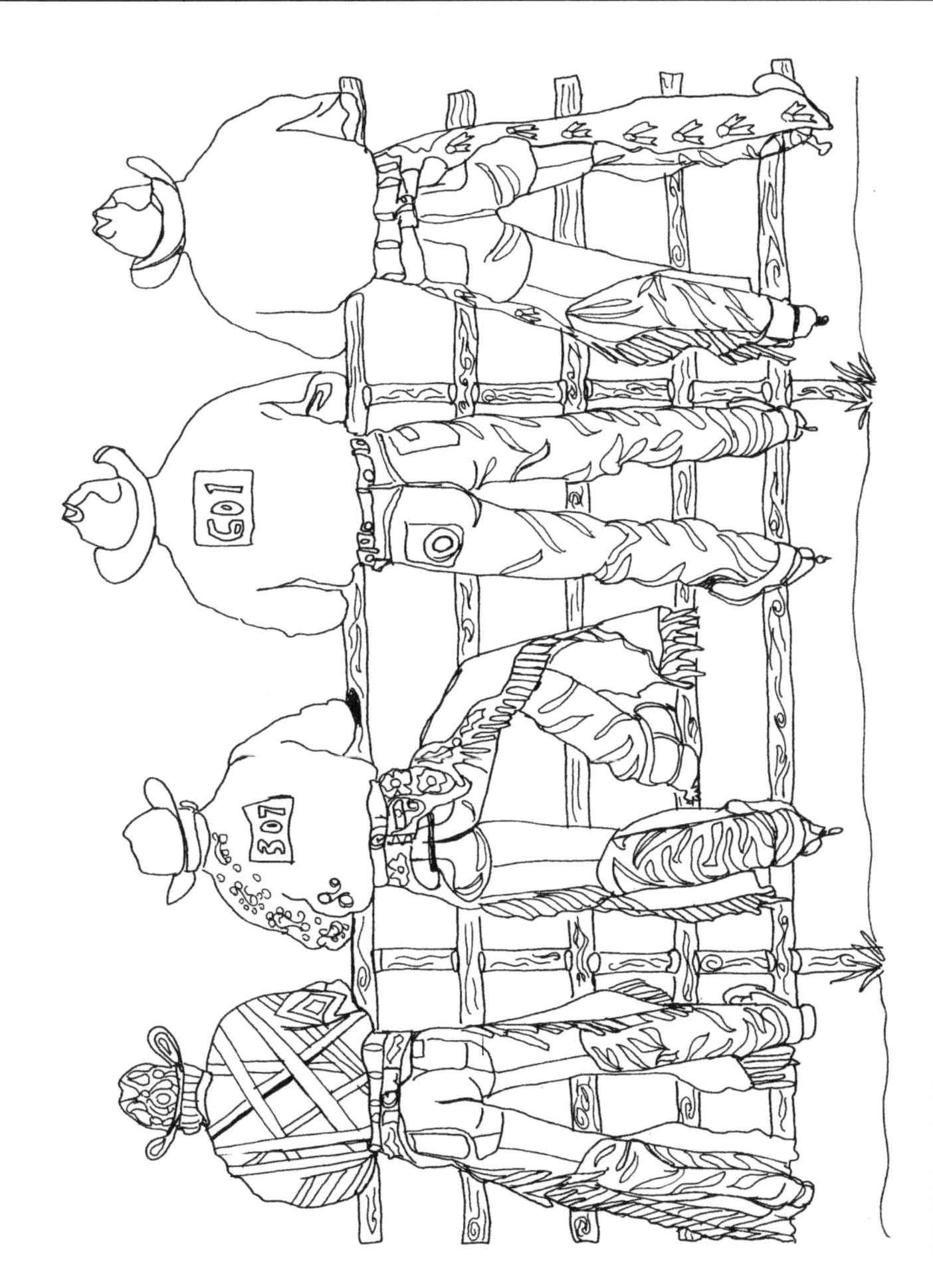

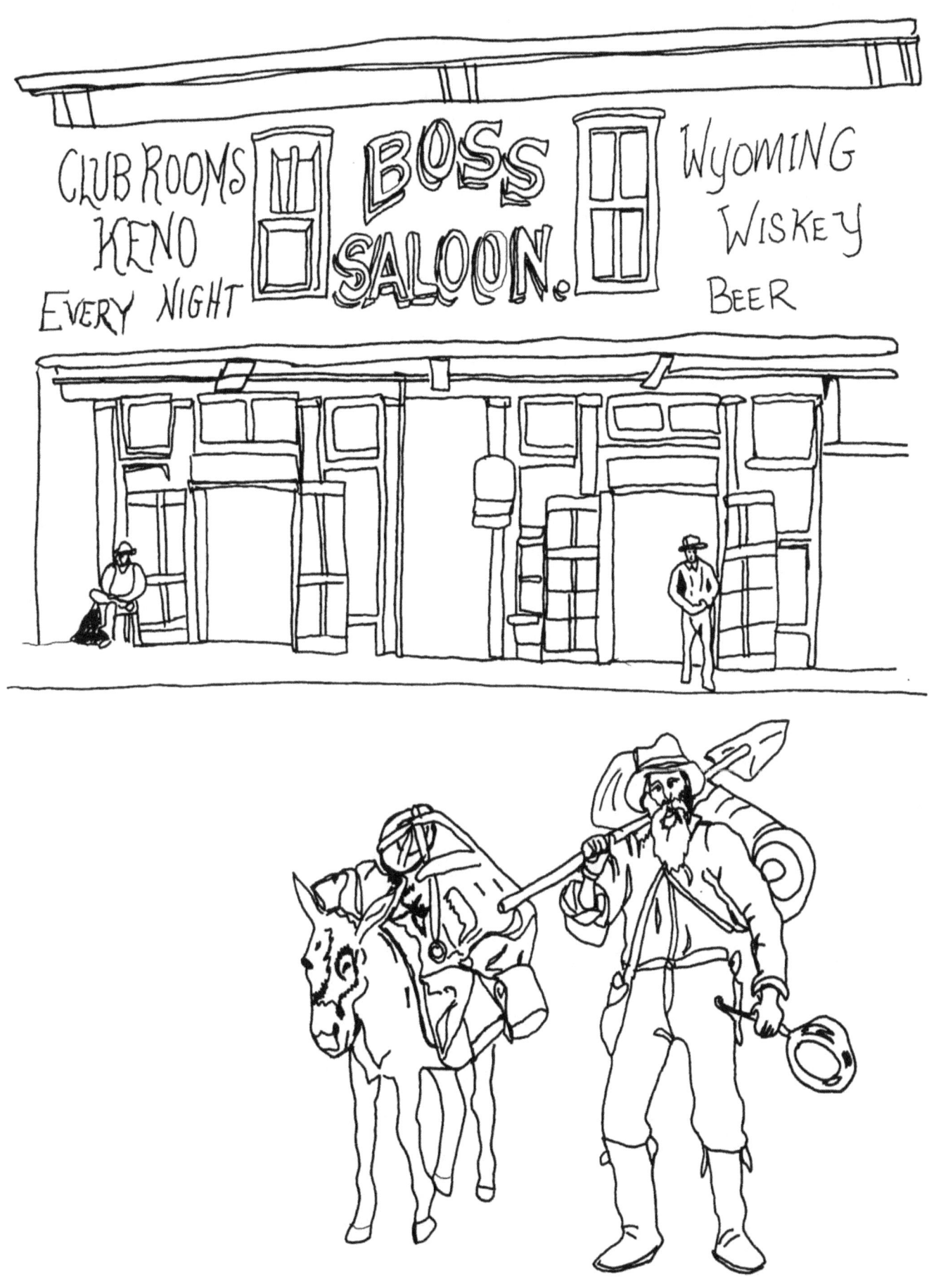

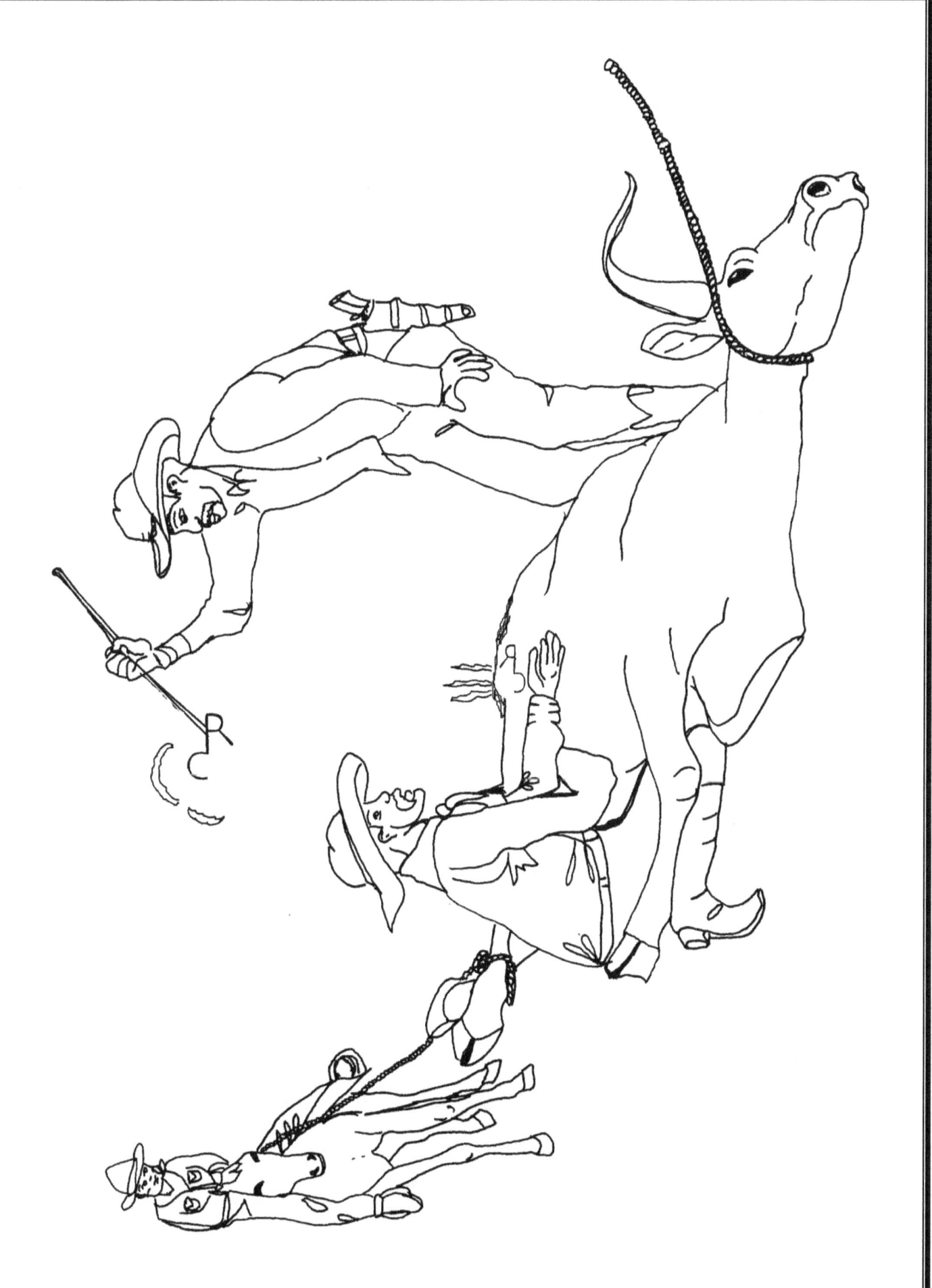

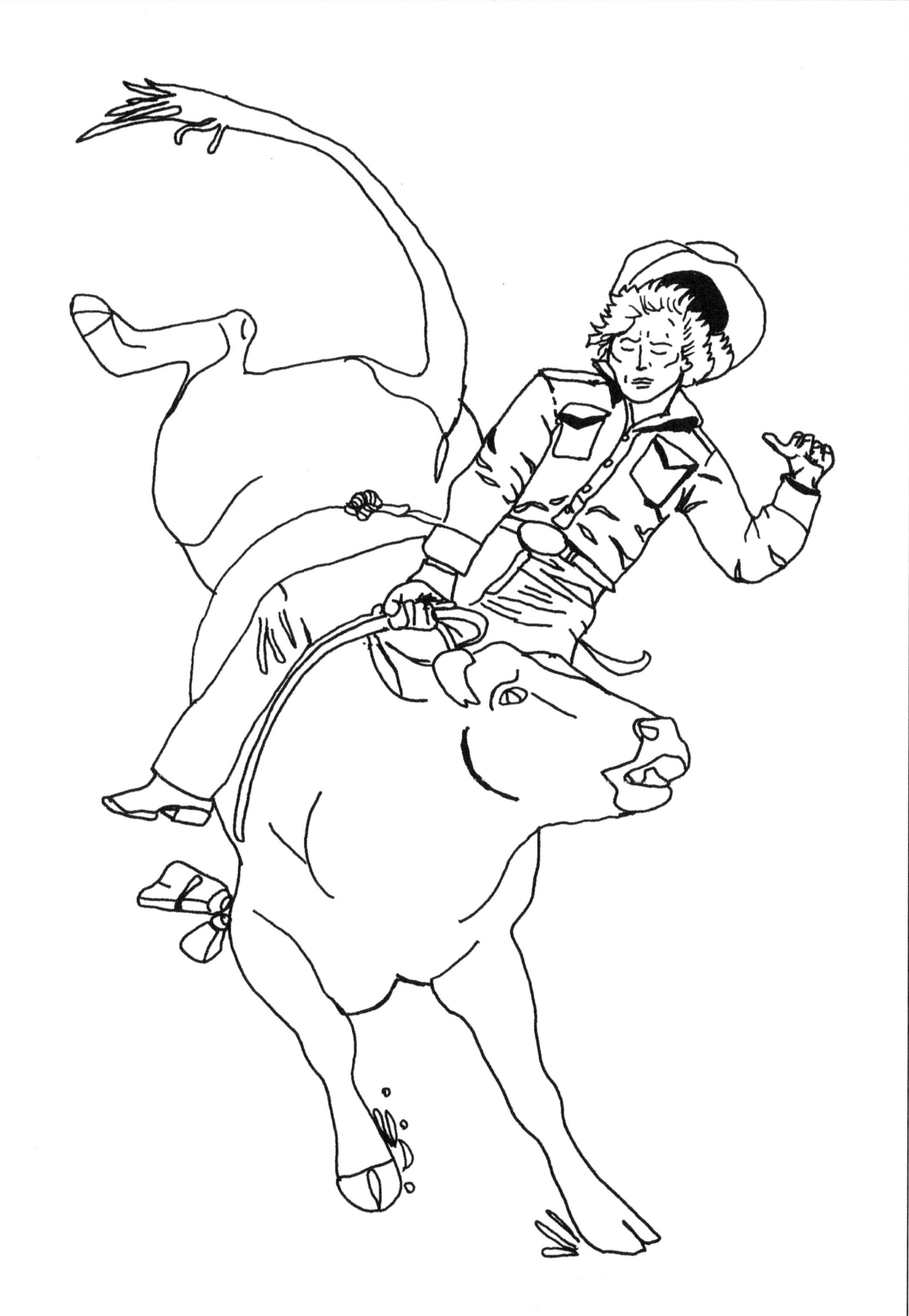

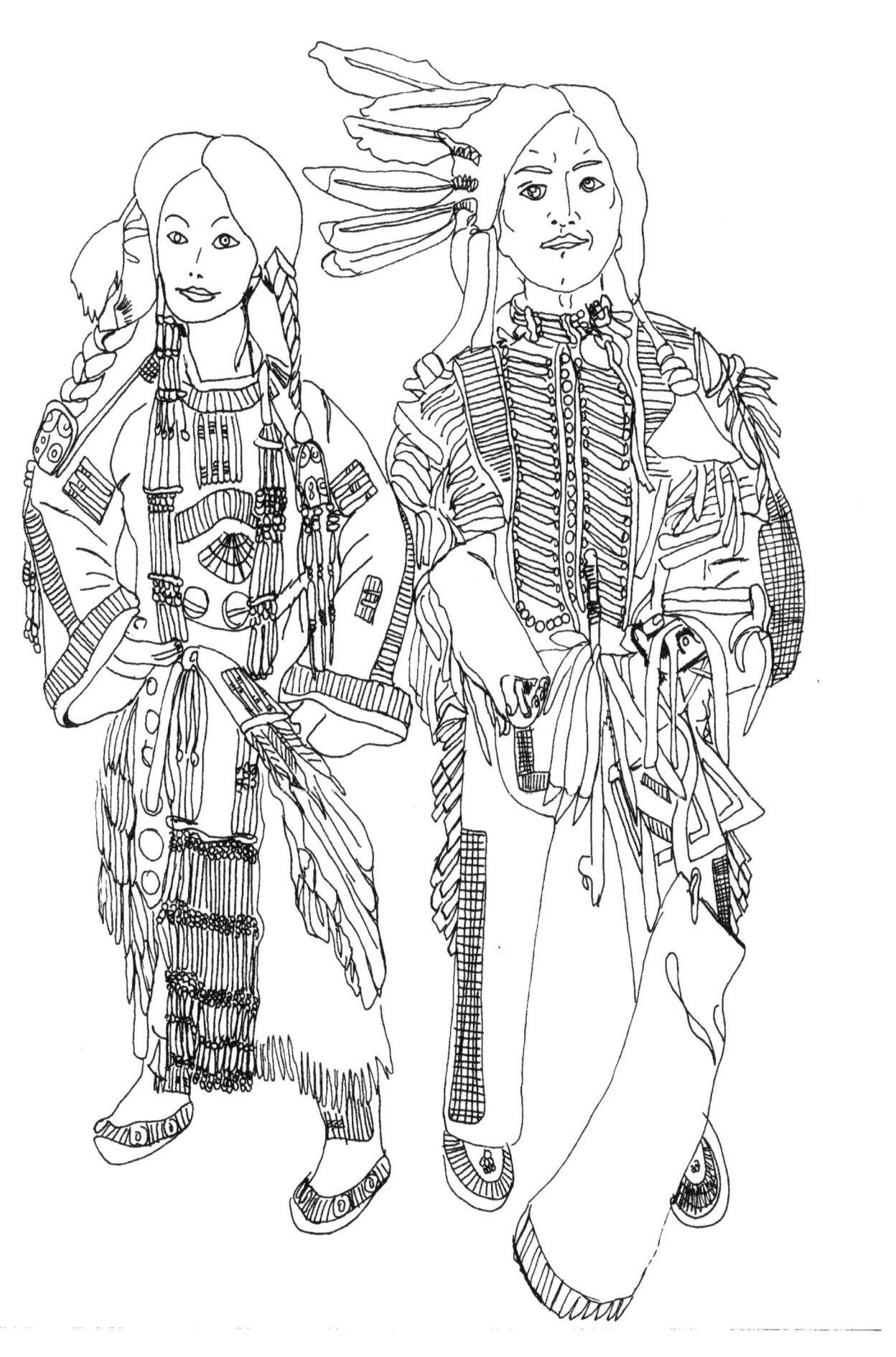

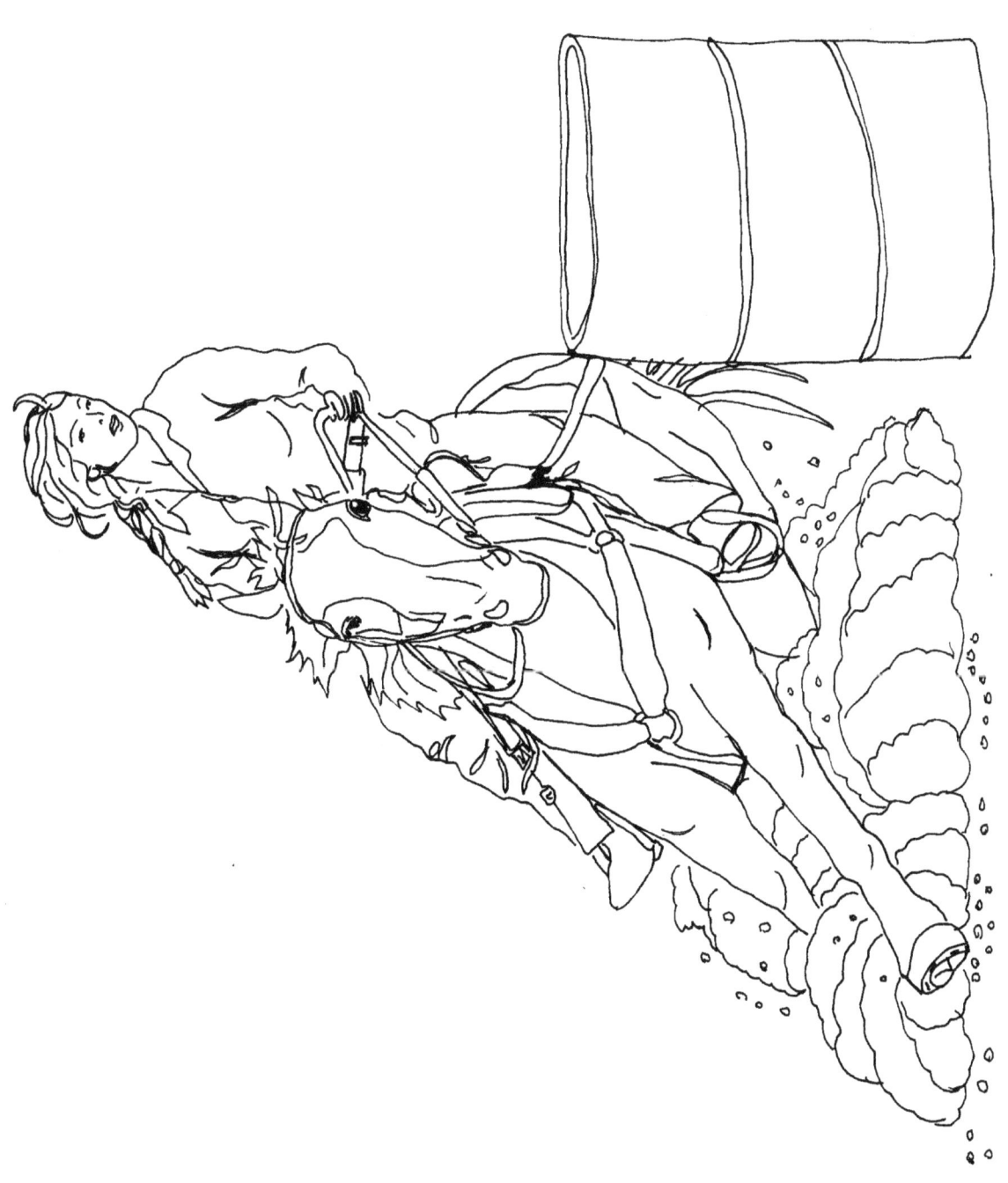

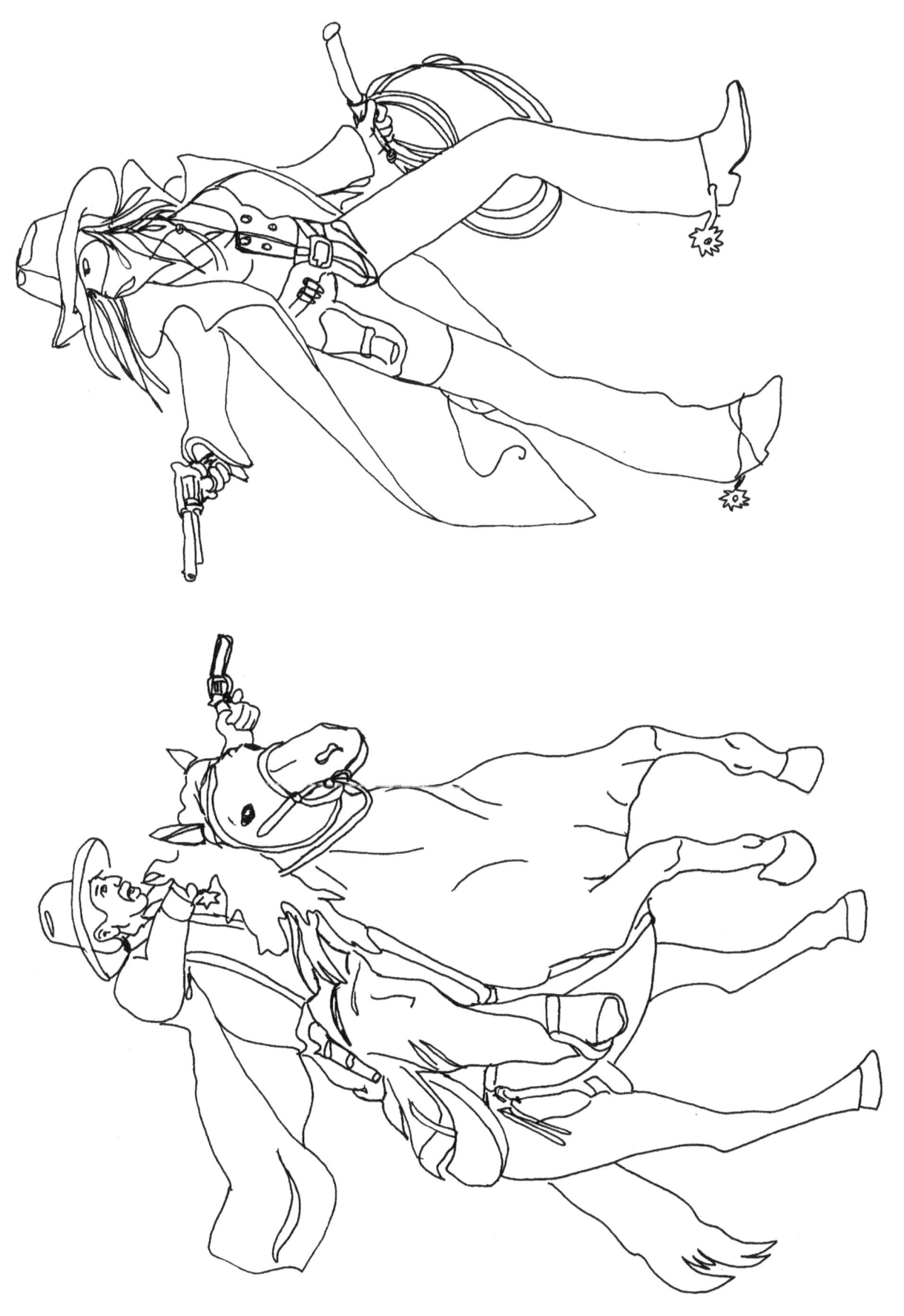

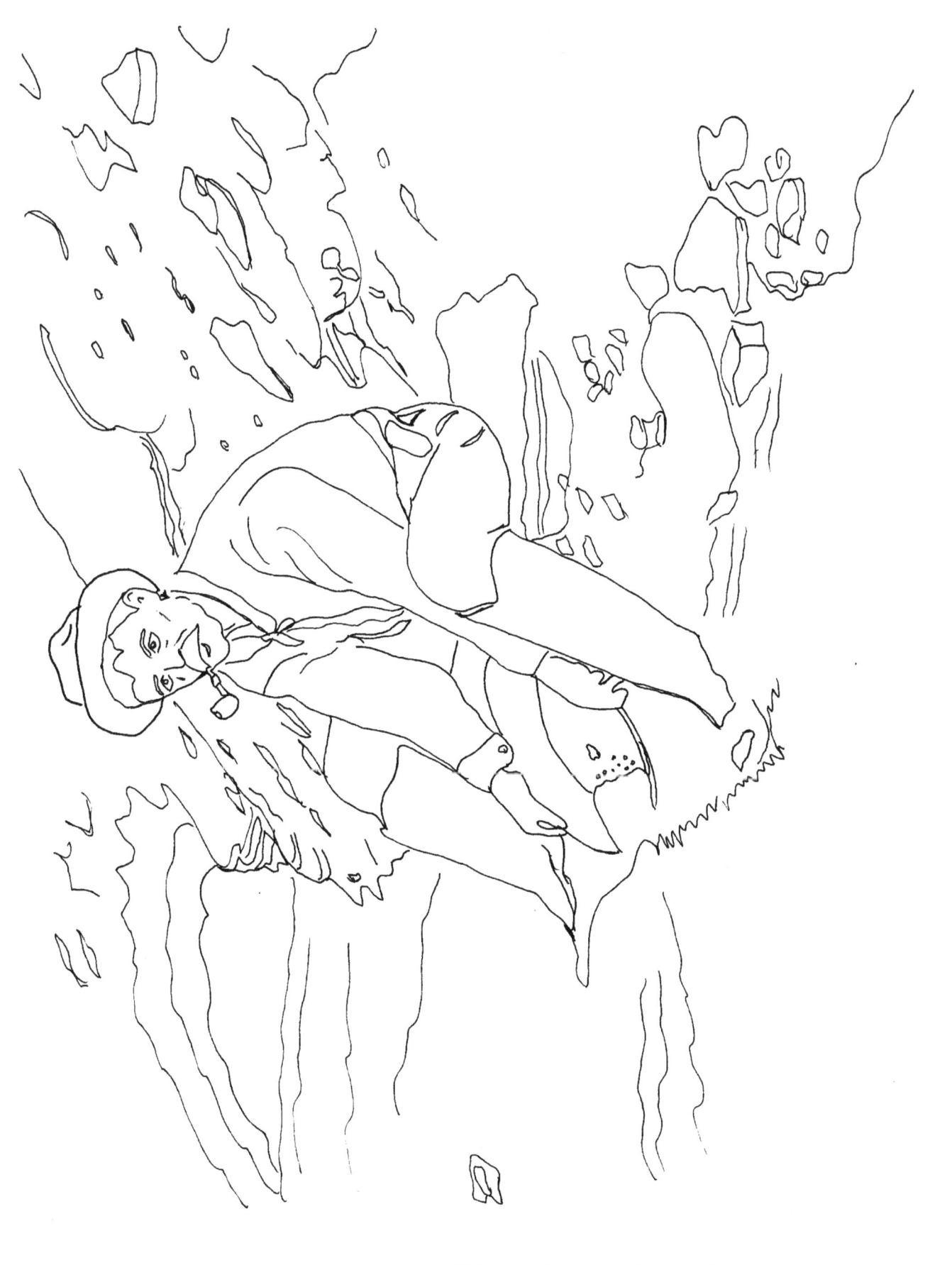

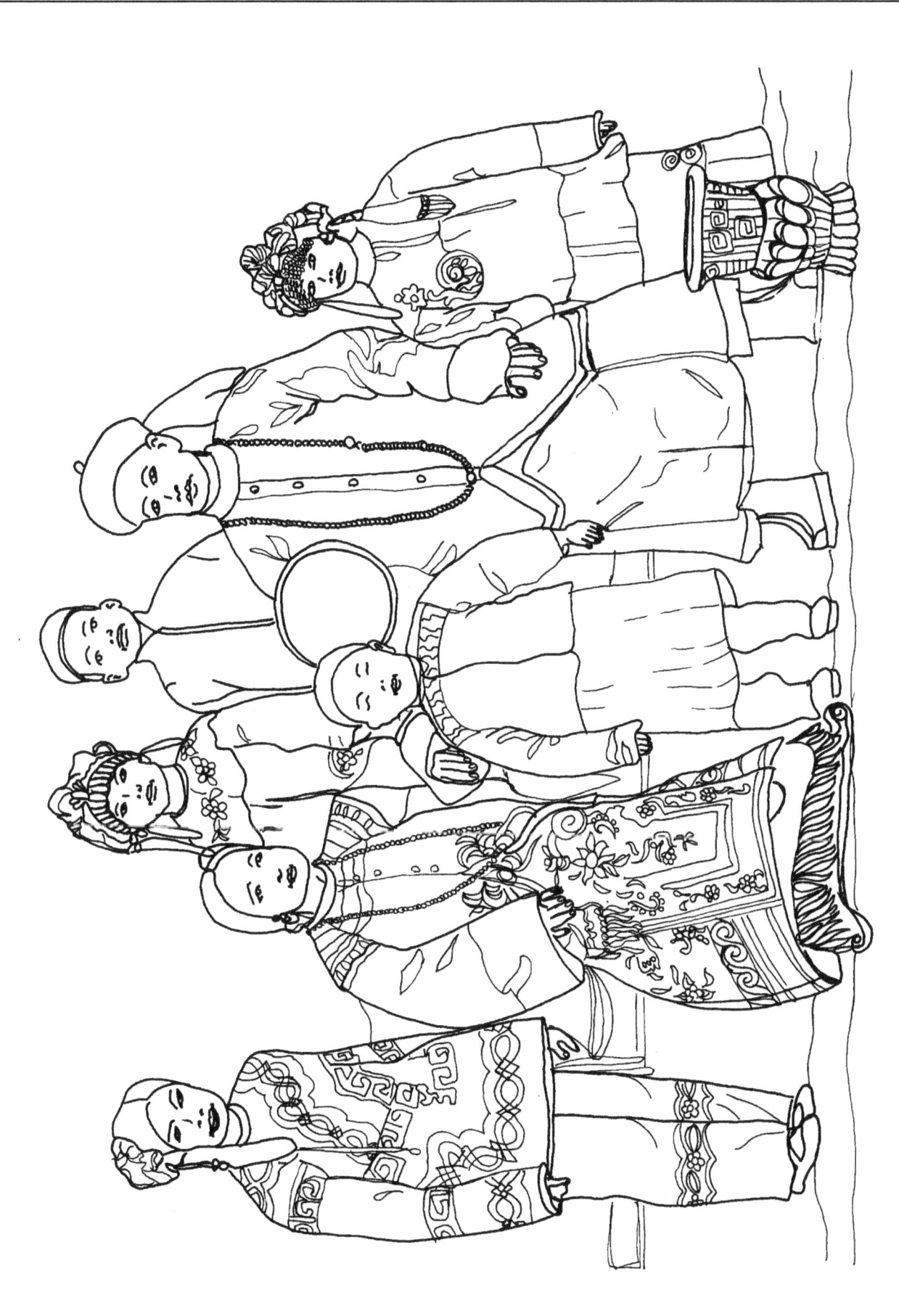

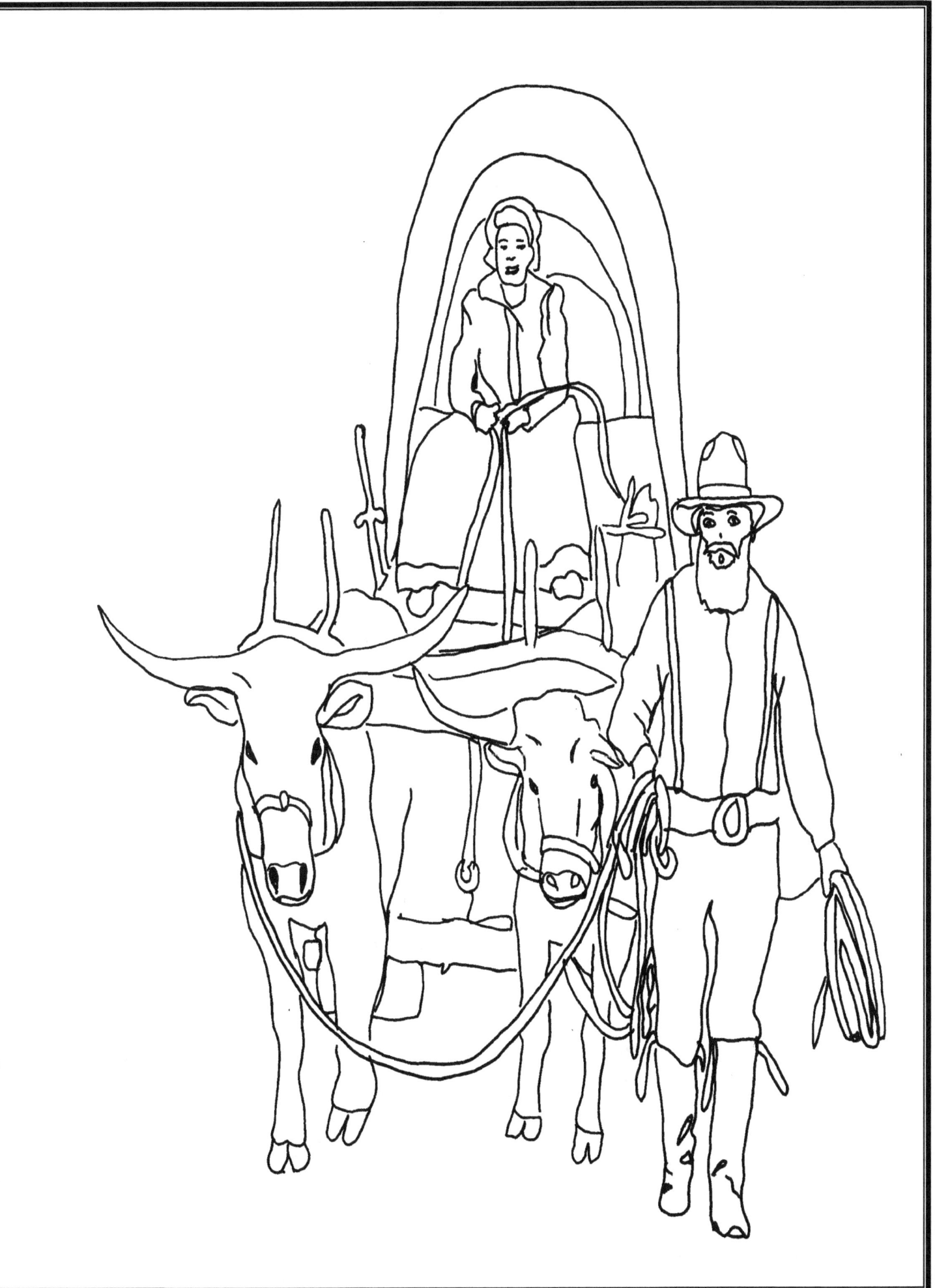

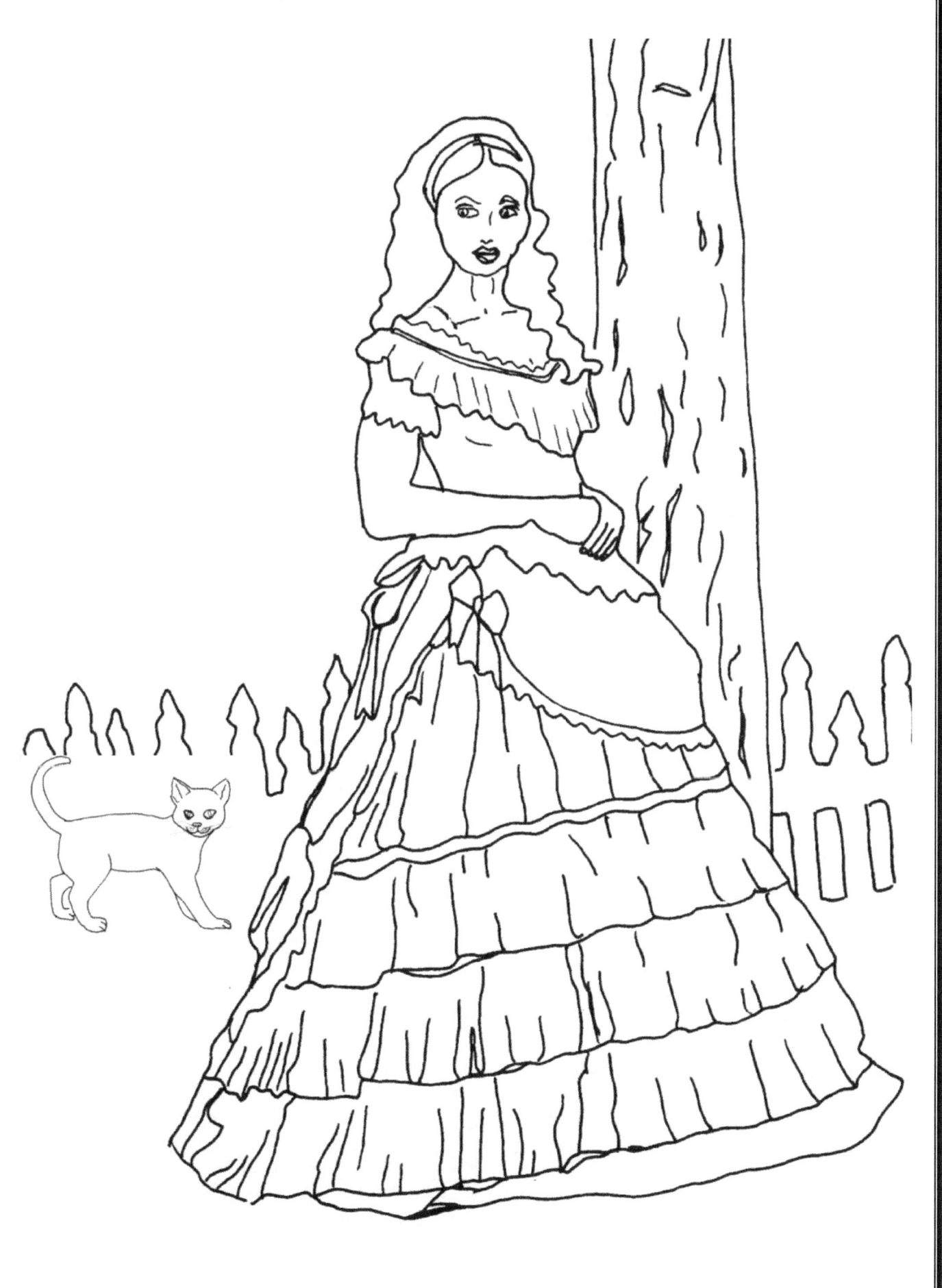

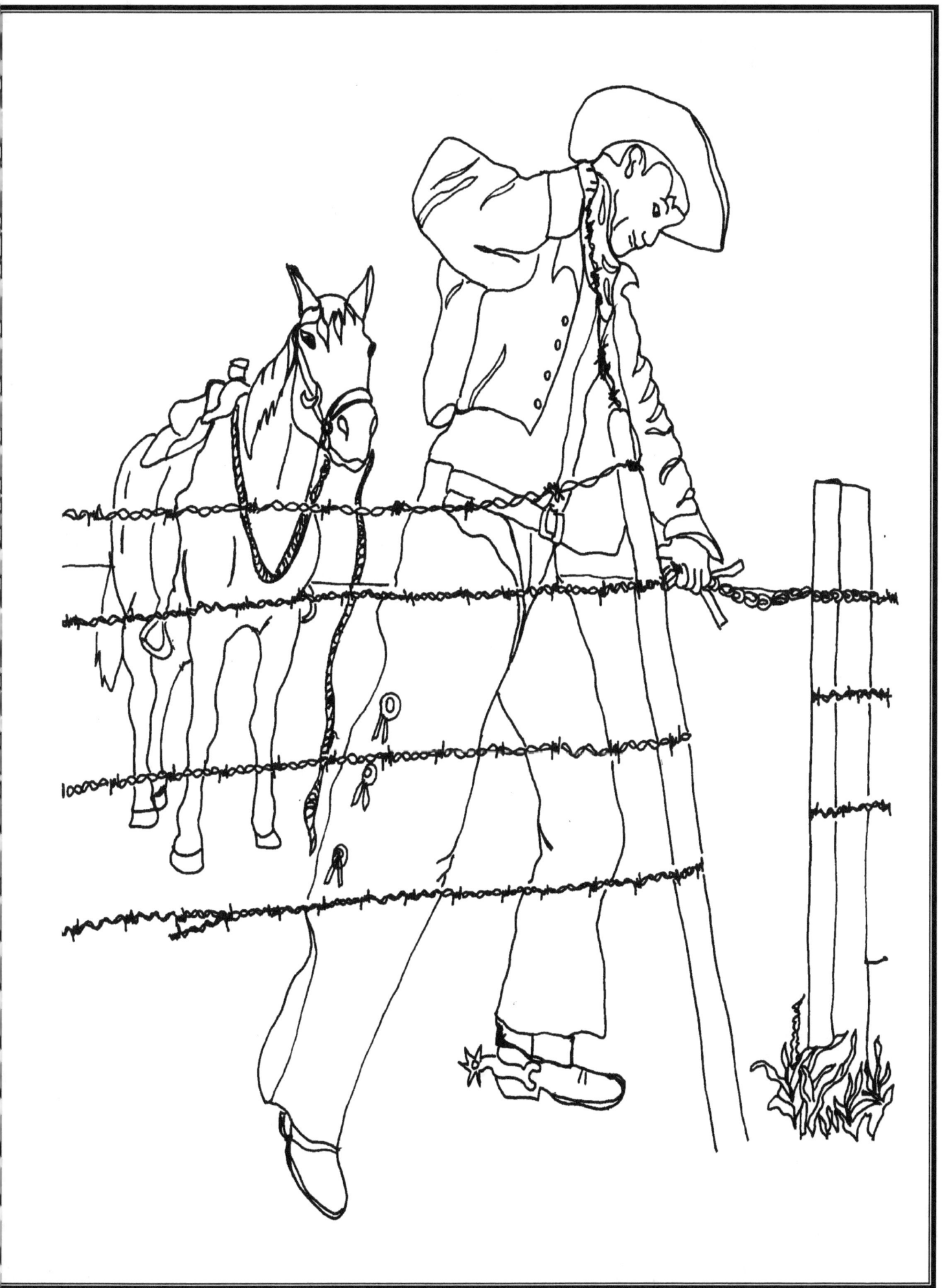

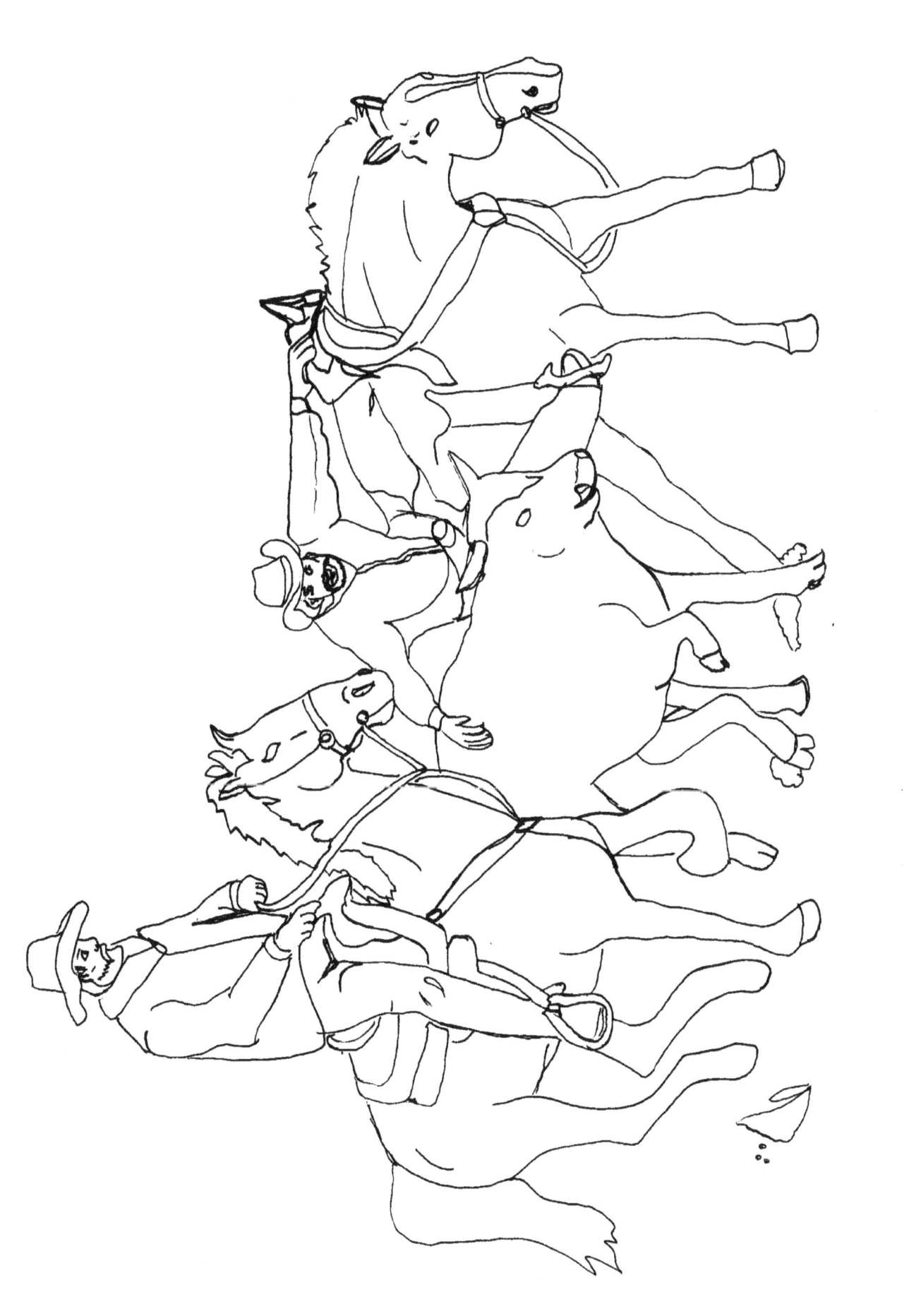

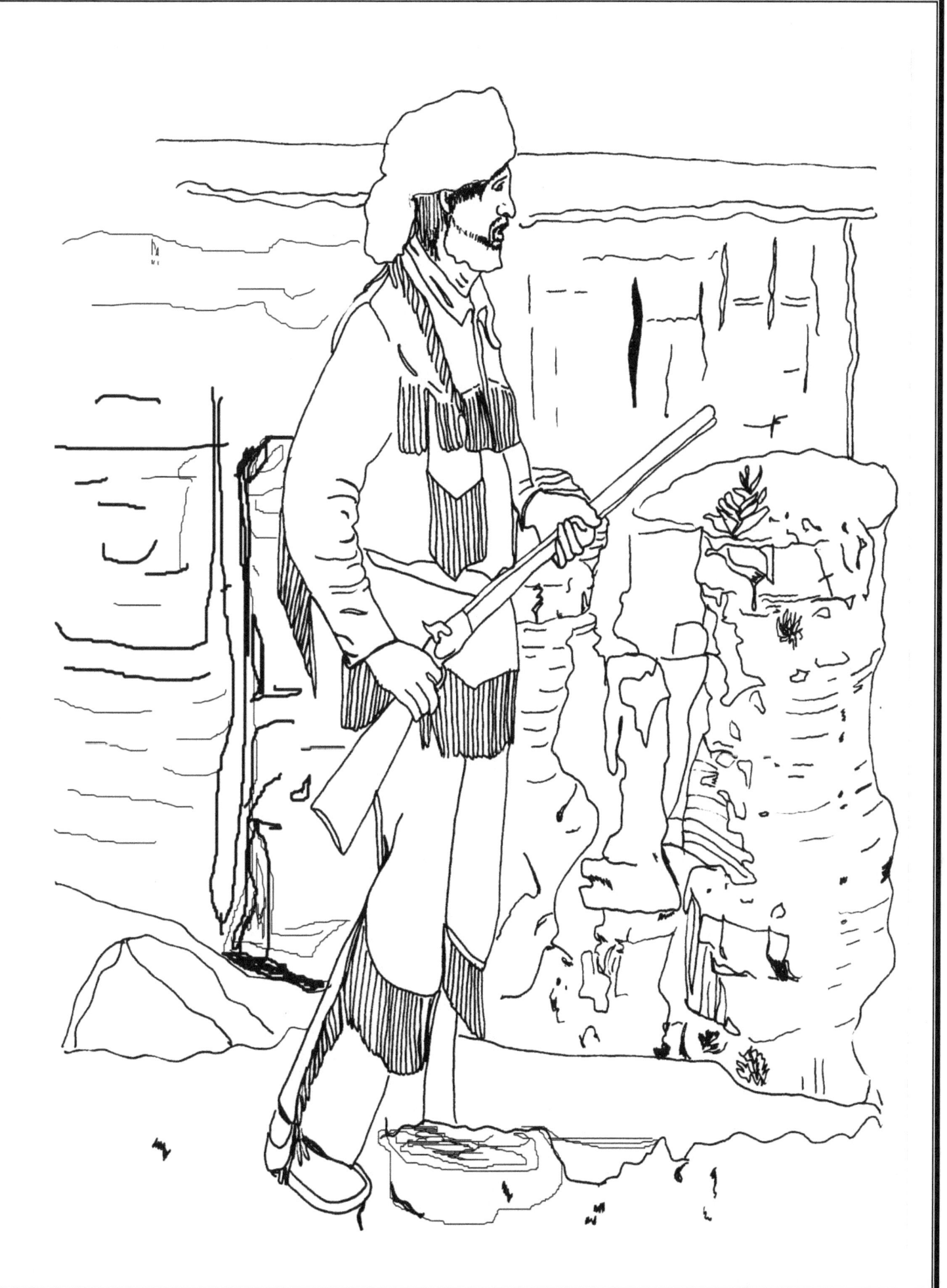

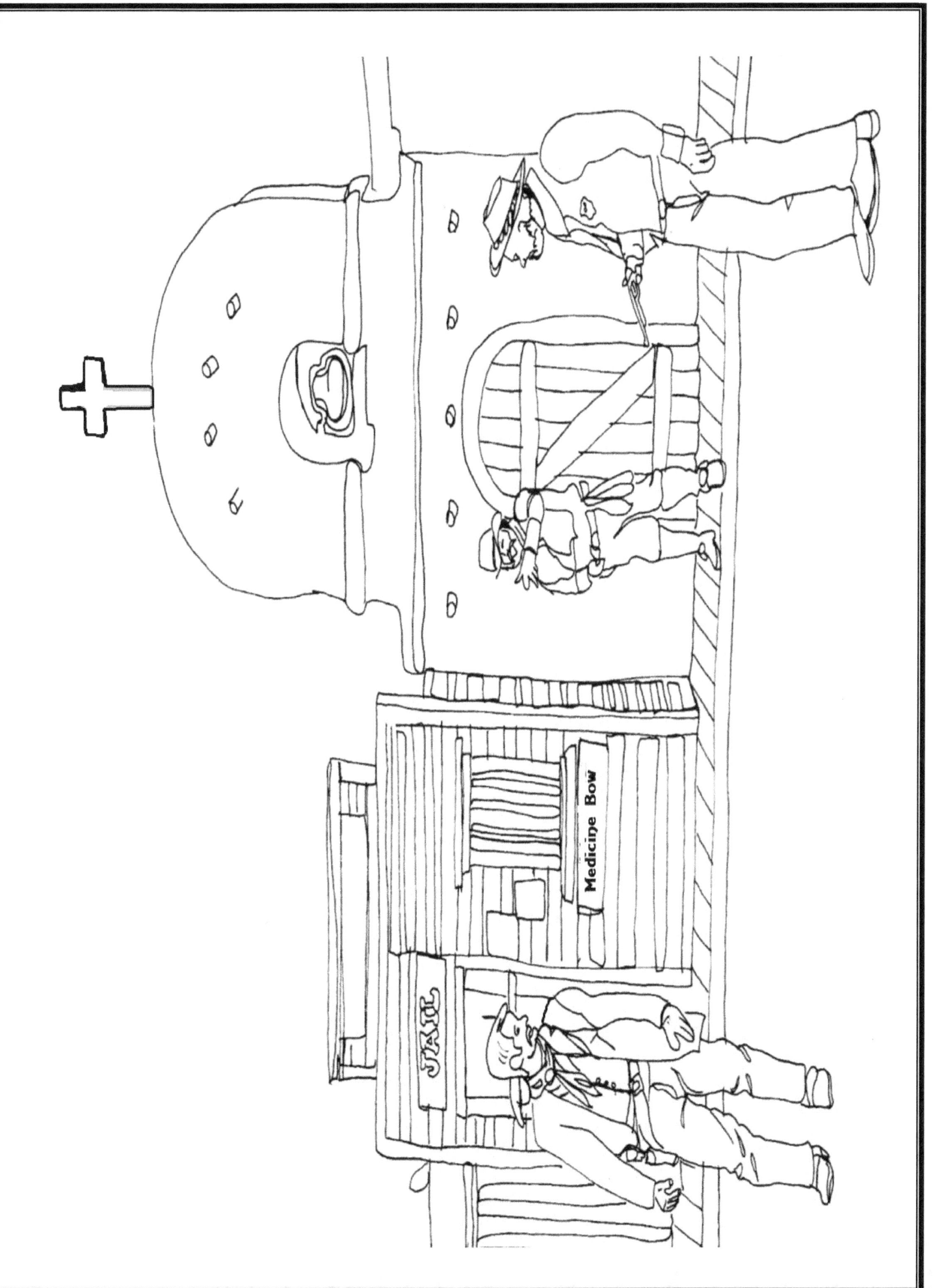

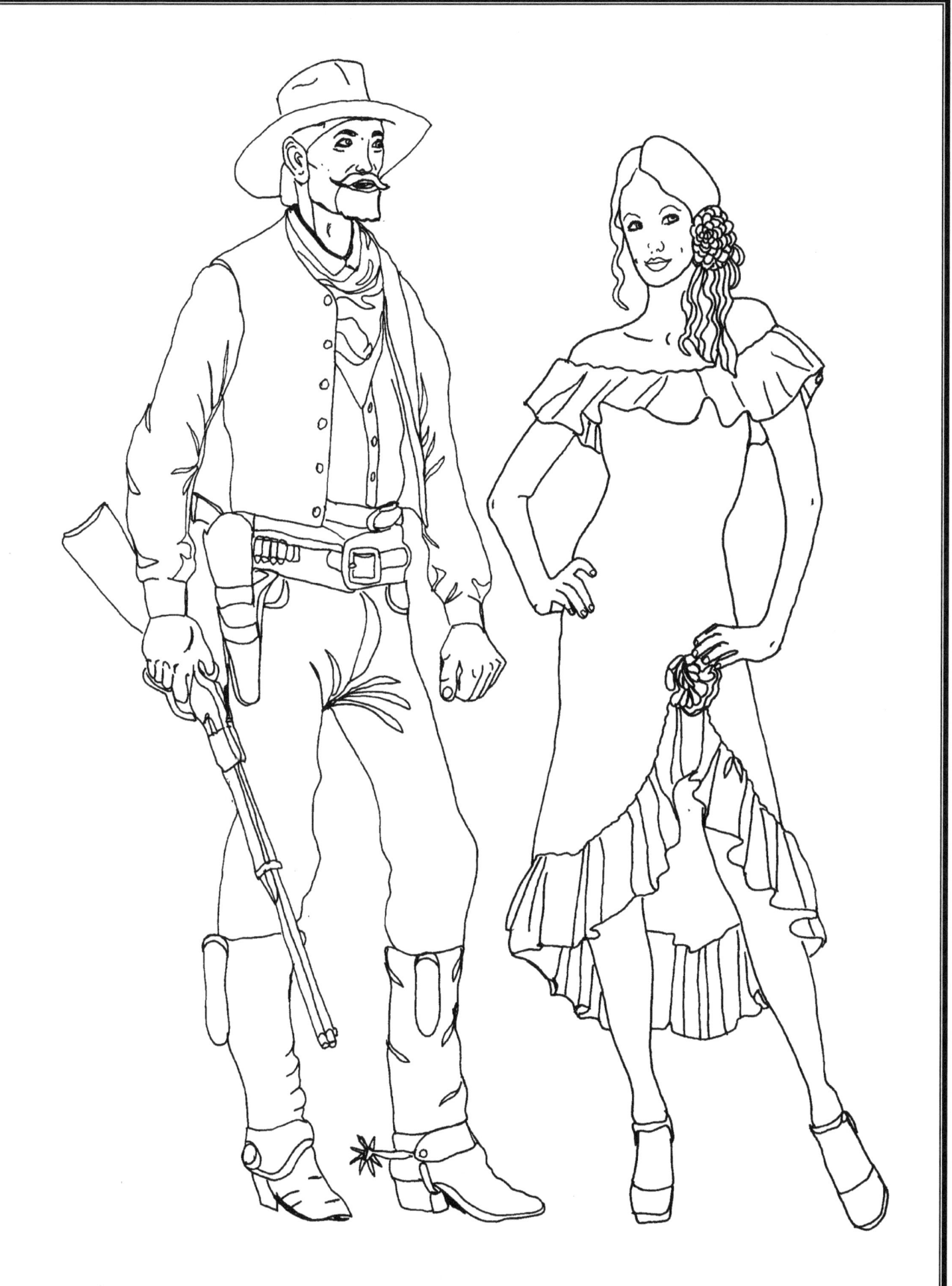

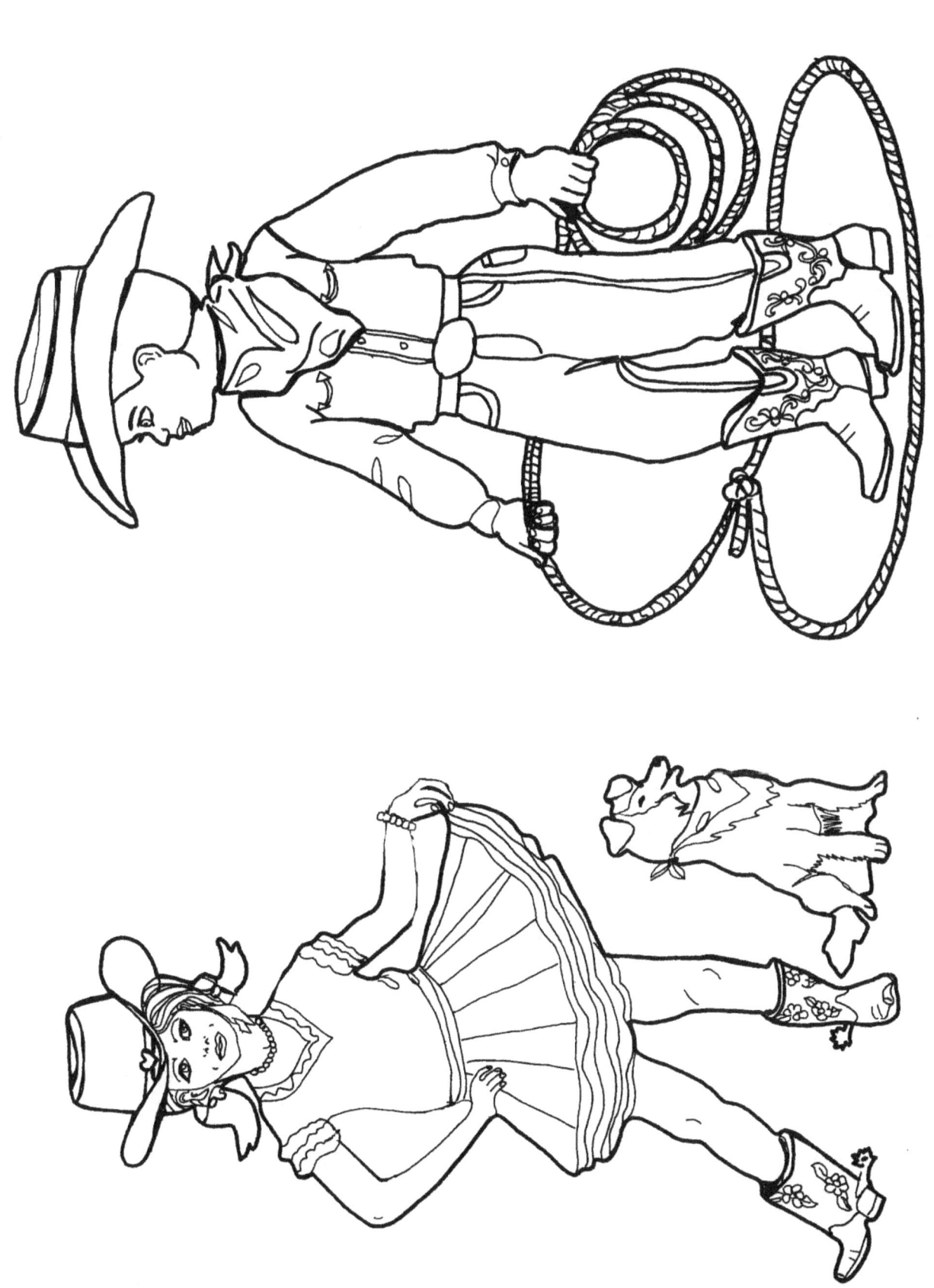

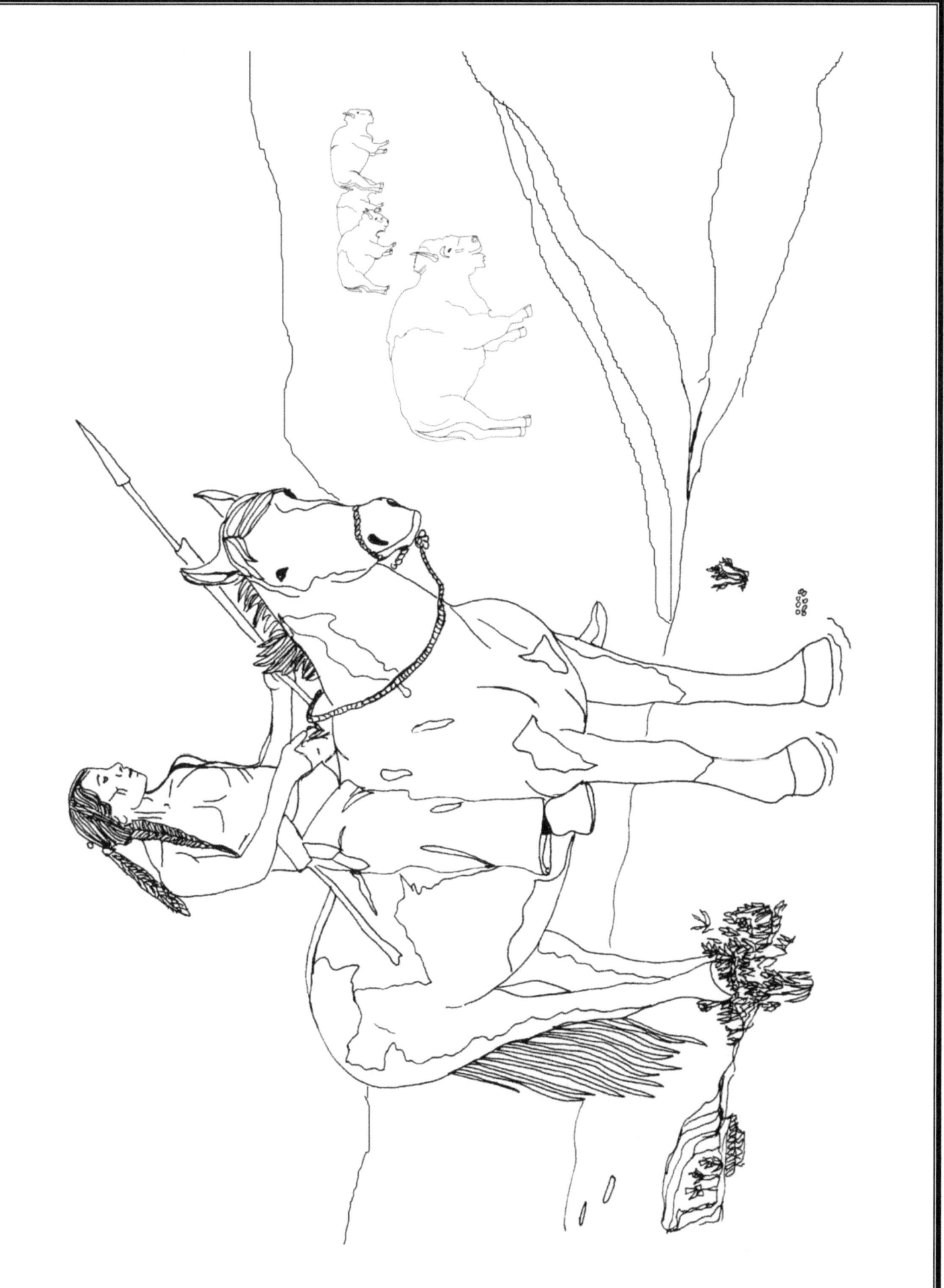

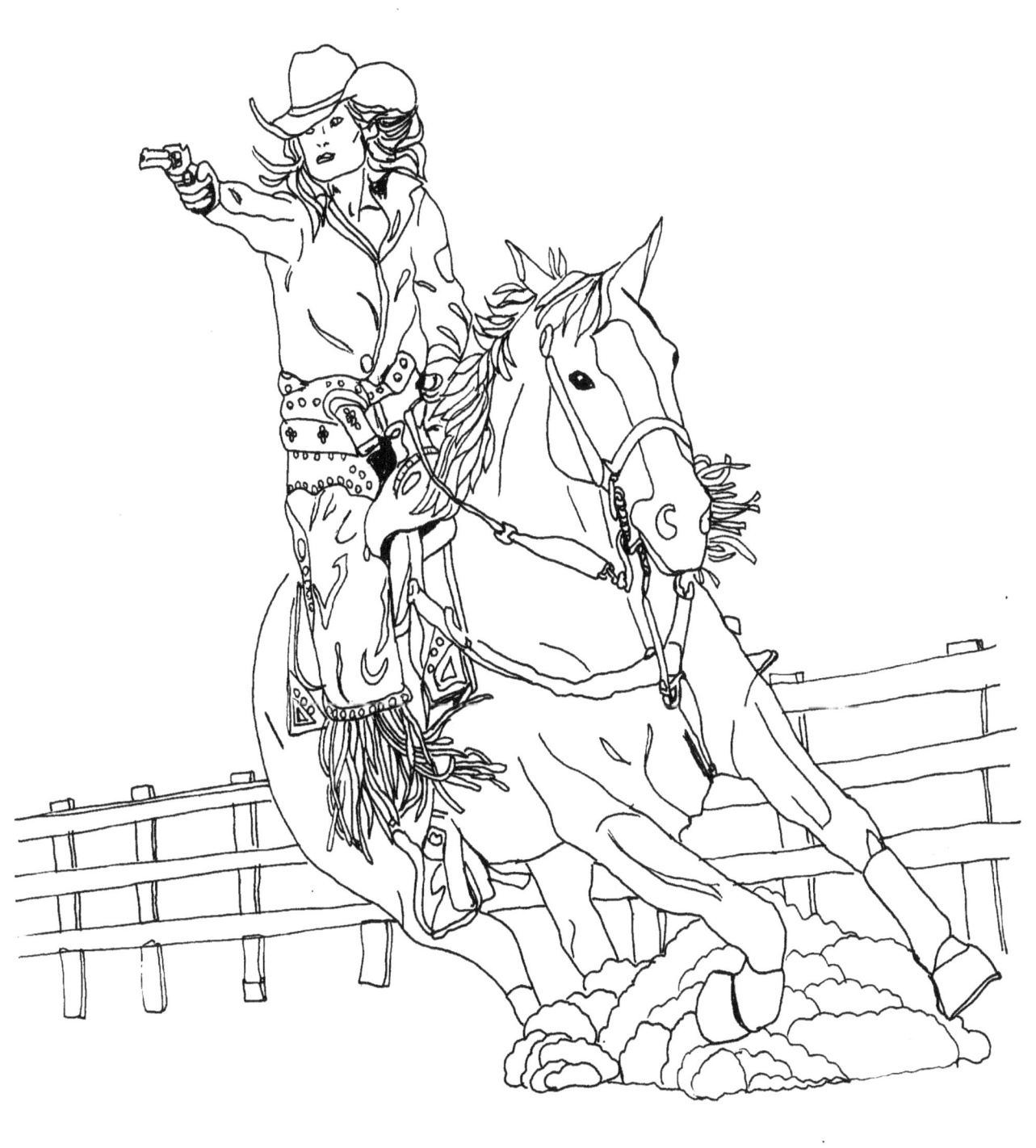

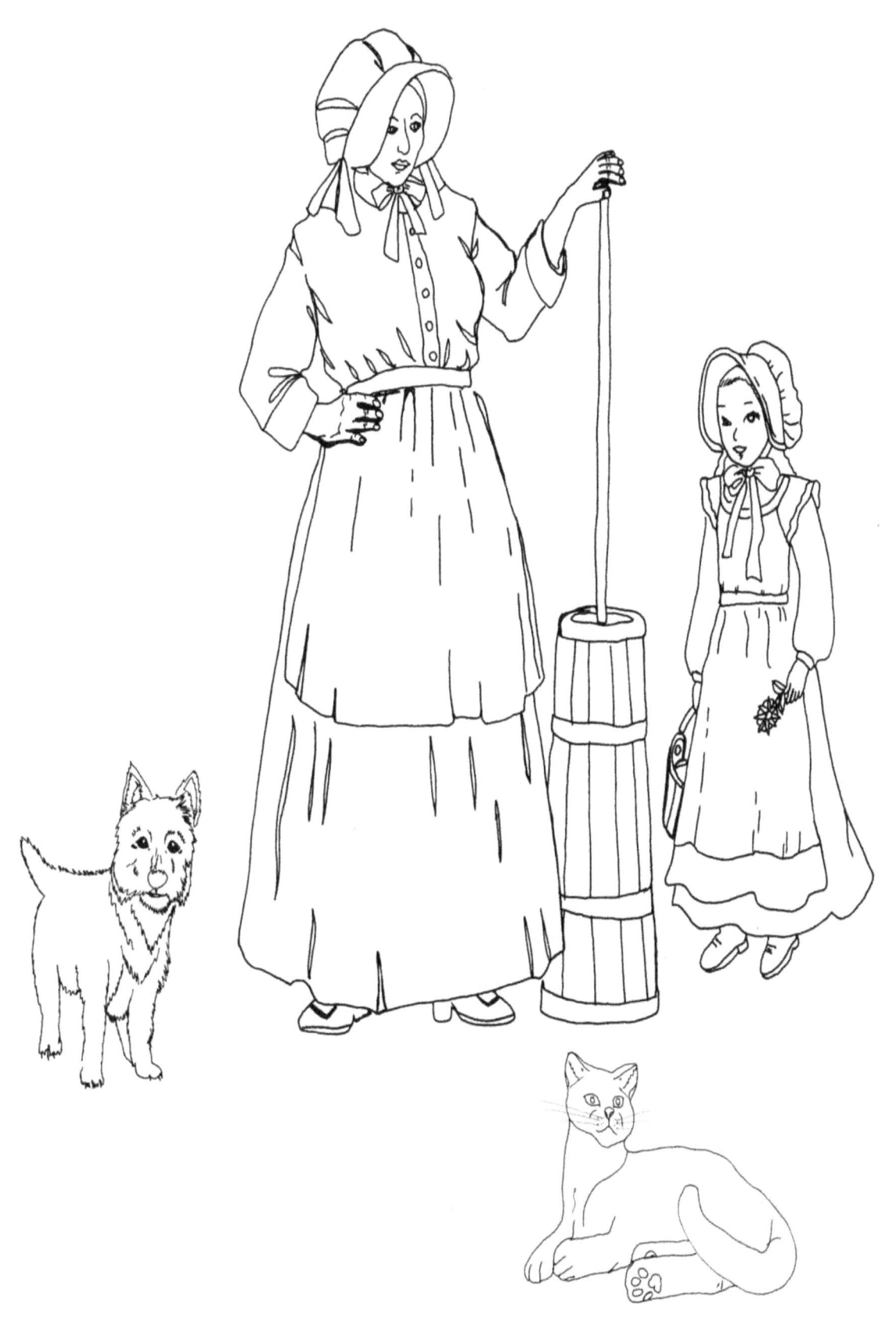

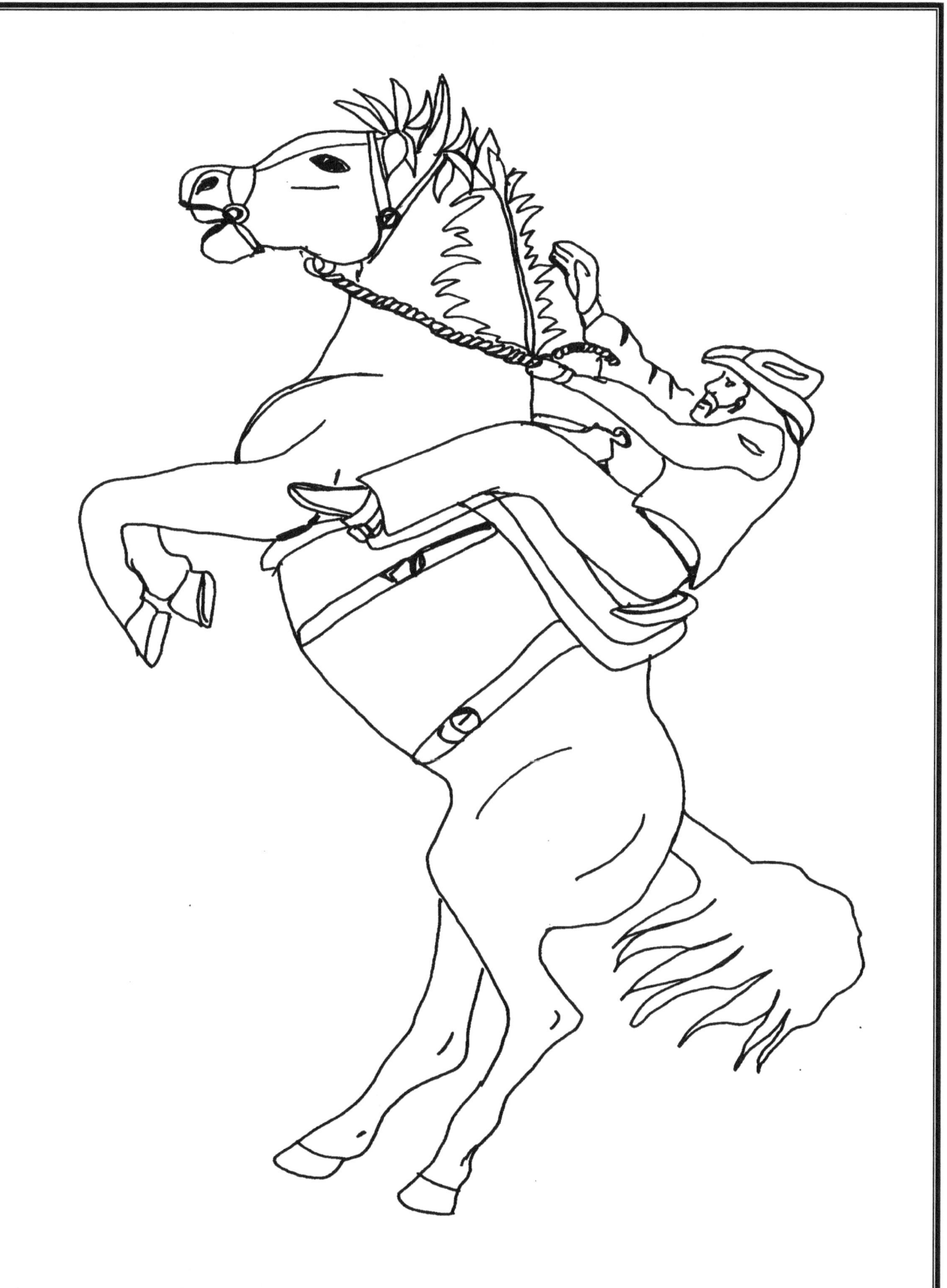

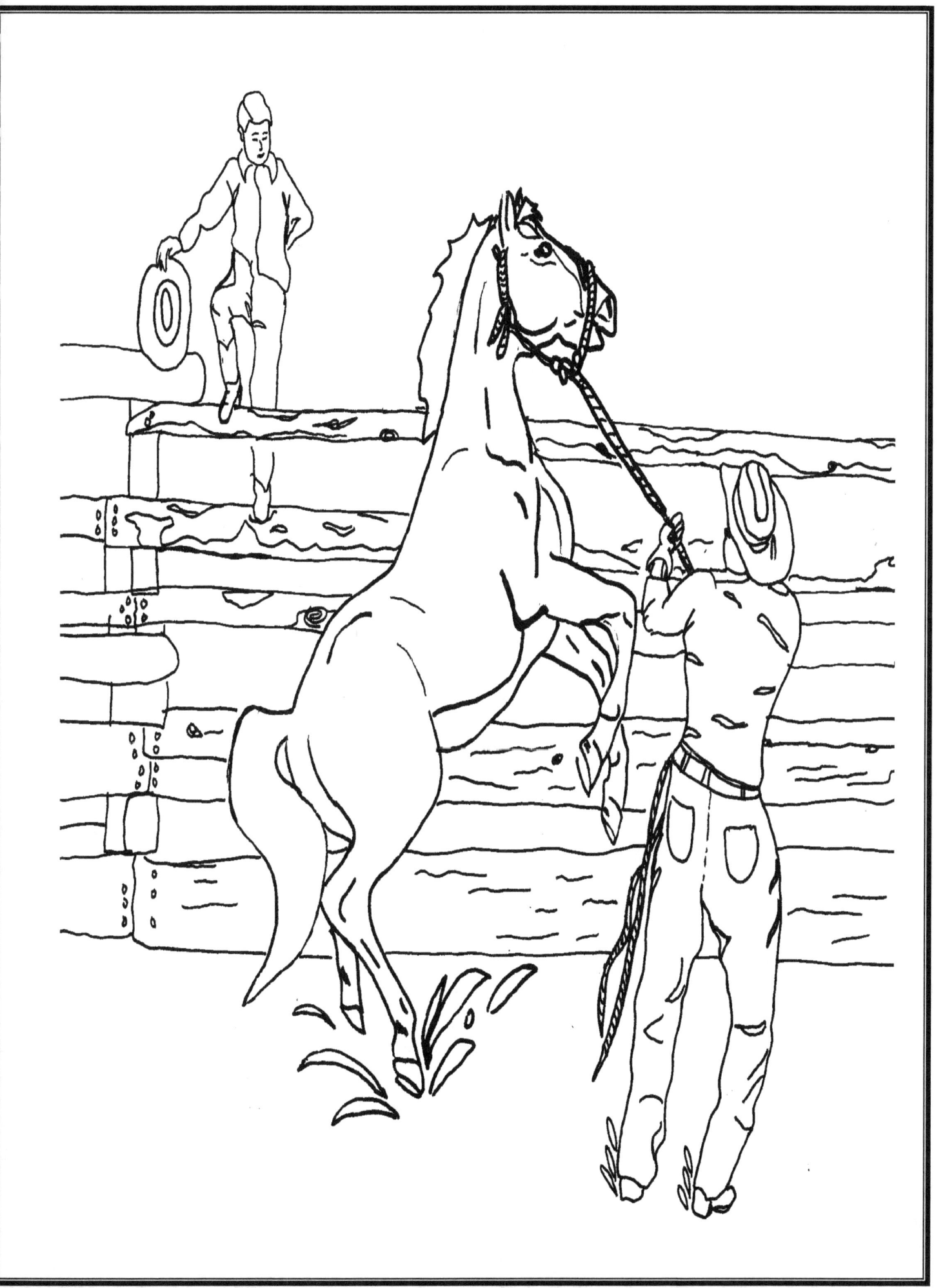

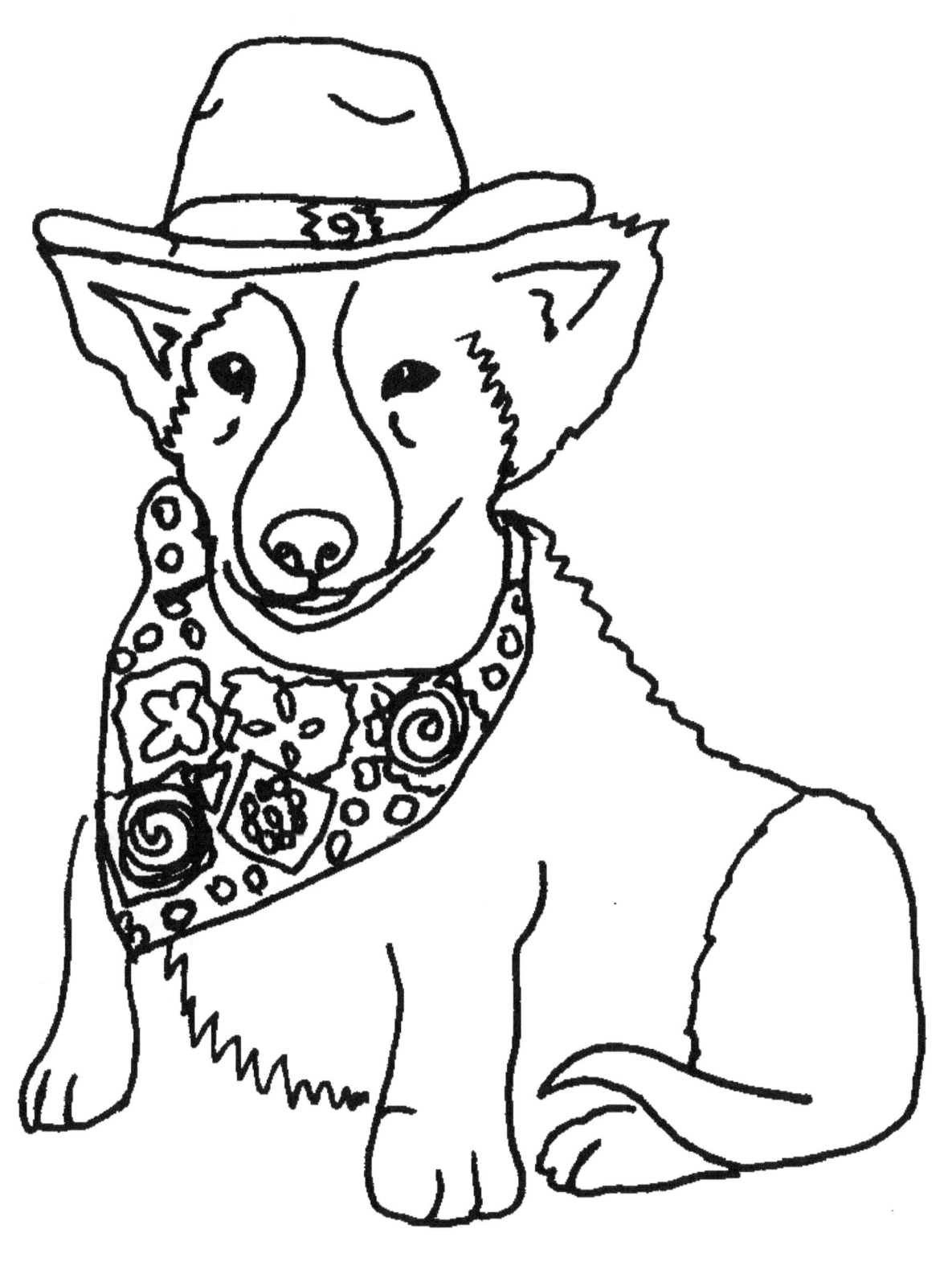

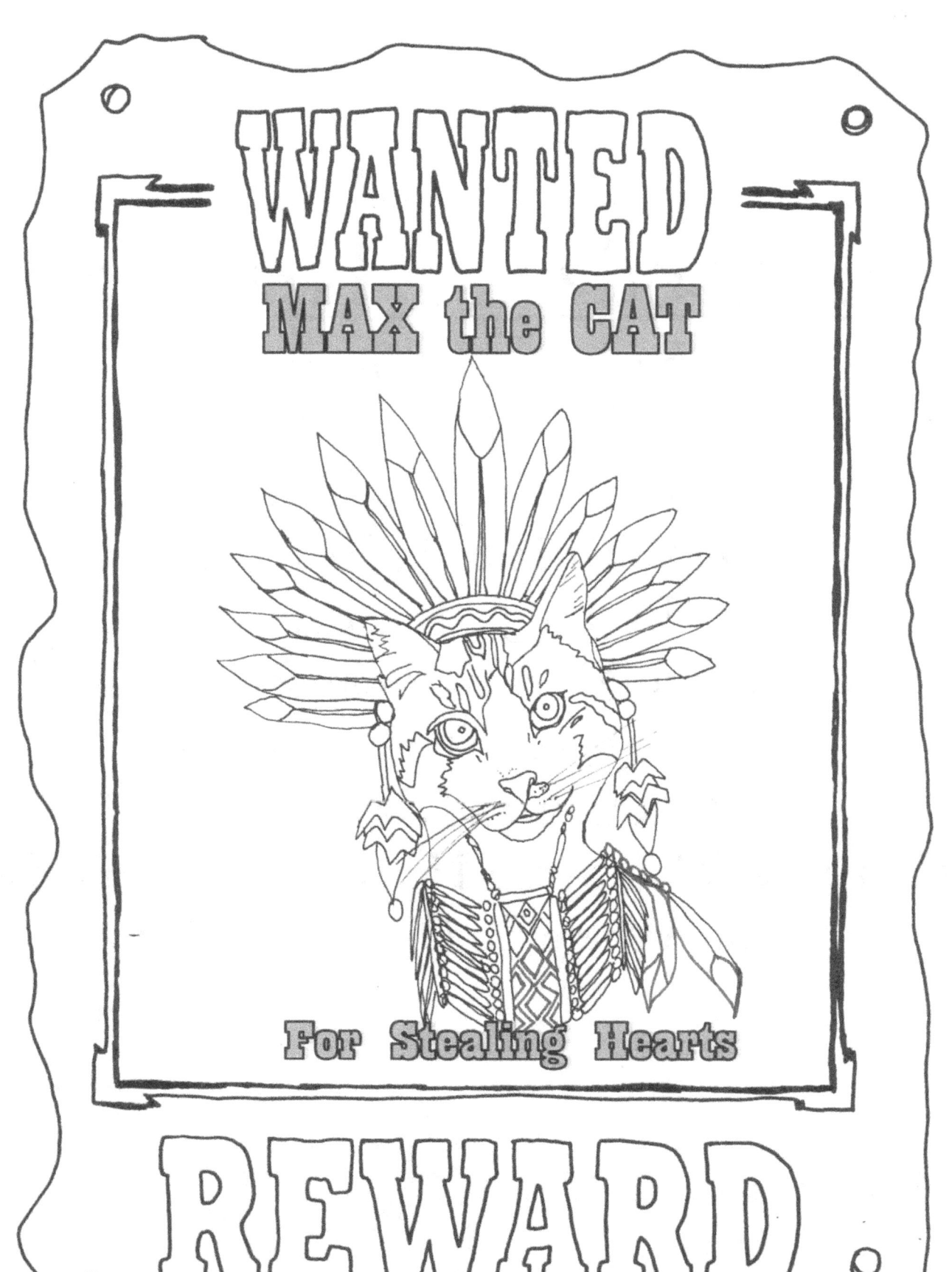

The Code Of The West

Live Each Day With Courage
Take Pride In Your Work
Always Finish What You Start
Do What Has To Be Done
Be Tough, But Fair
When You Make A Promise, Keep It
Ride For The Brand
Talk Less and Say More
Remember That Some Things Aren't For Sale
Know Where To Draw The Line

www.ingramcontent.com/pod-product-compliance
Lightning Source LLC
Chambersburg PA
CBHW080931170526
45158CB00008B/2244